SECRETS

SECRETS

WHY WAS I BORN IN THIS FAMILY?

SANDRA WALTERS

Published by Our Inspiring Stories, Texas
www.ourinspiringstories.com
Printed in the United States
Designed by Vince Pannullo

ISBN: 978-0-9995246-0-2

For information about bulk purchases, please contact Amazon.

CONTENTS

DEDICATION

I dedicate this book to my mother, sister, husband, and the Caver family because without them none of this would be possible.

ACKNOWLEDGMENTS

WRITING this book has been one of the hardest things I have attempted. Since I was a small child, I knew I was supposed to write a book about my experiences.

It wasn't until I had been married to my sweet husband for many years that I felt safe sharing my story. I would like to thank him for his unconditional love and support through my challenges.

I applaud my mother for being brave enough to give birth to me because I realize I could have been aborted.

I want to thank my big sister for always being there for me. I appreciate her encouragement and believing in me.

The Caver family deserves a special thank you for allowing me to be a part of their family. They introduced God's love to me, and for that, I am eternally grateful.

Thanks to all of the wonderful students I've had the opportunity to teach in twenty-plus years. They have made me a better person in so many ways. My Stripling, Coble, Jones, Davis, and Adams students have stretched me spiritually and professionally.

Finally, I thank God for turning my life around and giving me a "Happily Ever After".

CHAPTER 1

THE REVEAL

LILLY screamed in horror, "What is that?" as water streamed down her sister's legs. Caroline glanced back at Lilly with a mysterious expression on her face, but she didn't say a word. She had managed to keep her pregnancy a secret for nine months; however, when her water broke in front of her sister, she was exposed.

This young woman had neglected to receive prenatal care because she didn't feel she had anyone in her corner, so she harbored the news inside. When she initially shared this information with the father, he promised to help her, but he hadn't been seen since that day. She didn't believe her family would understand. Therefore, she struggled with this secret alone. Still, she was brave enough to carry this baby until it was time to deliver. Nervously and quietly, she began packing her bags while her sister asked questions and tried to console her. Caroline changed her clothes and gathered her bags. Lilly agreed to clean up her mess as she prepared to venture down the street.

On that freezing cold winter morning in January,

this petite, caramel-colored female in her early twenties opened the door of her mother's house and headed outside. In urgency all bundled up, she strolled briskly down the street with the contractions coming stronger and more frequently. To those watching, she looked like a wobbly fat person walking, stopping, and bending over every few minutes. After traveling what seemed to be a mile, she finally reached the neighborhood convenience store. She explored the items in her purse in search of a quarter. Once she found the shiny silver coin, Caroline placed the money into the pay phone slot. Then, she dialed a number she had written on a piece of white scratch paper. Positioning the phone to her ear, she listened for someone to hear her request.

The operator said, "Hello, this is the Yellow Cab Company. How may I assist you?"

Caroline replied, "Please send a cab to 501 Baltimore."

The woman answered, "We are sending one now."

"Thank you," Caroline groaned. Next, she waited outside in the cold for about thirty minutes praying, "Lord, please don't let this baby come before the cab arrives." Finally, she saw the yellow-checkered sedan coming down the street. She thought, *Thank goodness! I didn't have this baby in this parking lot.* As the cab approached and stopped in a parking space, she gently moved to the vehicle and opened the door while placing her bags inside.

The driver asked, "What's your destination?"

Caroline answered, "John Peter Smith Hospital."

While she journeyed to the hospital, back at home her mother and five siblings were discussing the situation. Questions and comments filled the house. Her brothers and sisters shouted, "I didn't know she was pregnant. I thought she was getting a little plump. Who's the daddy?"

Their mother responded with an agitated voice, "I bet it's Fat Daddy's baby, and he ain't no good. I told that girl to stay away from that boy, but she is so hard headed. How is she gonna take care of another baby? Denise is only fifteen months and still in diapers. She'll have to pack her stuff and move out because we don't have enough room for another baby. I'm not running a daycare."

After a few hours of conversation and preparation, Eddie, Lilly, Big Mama, Denise, and Bernice got in the car and traveled to the hospital. Once they arrived, everyone headed to the front desk and the attendant asked, "May I help you?"

Eddie stated, "Caroline Baker had a baby here this morning, and we're trying to find her room."

The receptionist said, "Let me see," while she looked at a sheet of paper with a list of names and room numbers. "Caroline is in the Labor and Delivery Unit on the third floor. Her room number is 315. Take the elevator by the gift shop and follow the numbers on the wall; once you get to Labor and Delivery, turn right." Eddie led the family through the hospital.

When they finally approached room 315, he knocked on the door and whispered, "Hello, we're here." Everyone eased in and immediately started to inspect the baby except for Denise. She ran to her mother while the others simply pretended as if everything was normal as they always did. Silence was the method of dealing with difficult situations. It was extremely awkward, but no one asked any questions. They just passed the new baby around like she was a rag doll. She had huge curls, chubby cheeks, and perfect brown skin. She looked like a "Mexican" baby. At least that's what Caroline said.

Lilly asked, "What's her name?"

"Shannon Ann Baker," Caroline replied.

"That's a nice name," responded Lilly.

After staying at the hospital for about two hours, the family decided to go home.

However, Caroline remained in the hospital for about two days and had her tubes tied. She wasn't going to make this mistake again. Eventually, she returned home with her brand new baby girl. She really didn't know how she was going to take care of her two girls, but she was determined to do the best she knew how with her tenth-grade education.

CHAPTER 2

THE GRIND

ONCE my mom recovered from childbirth, she went back to work as a maid in the housekeeping department of the Roadway Inn Motel, and she also cleaned rich, white people's homes on the weekends. After some time, she enrolled in school to obtain a nursing aide certificate to work in nursing homes. While working an eight-hour shift, she studied from these extremely large books nonstop, day in and out, trying to obtain her goal. Following many months of hard work, she finally received the certificate. Then, she could really provide for us.

She purchased extravagant items for us from Payless and Kmart. Those were our favorite stores; we thought we were fancy shopping at such exclusive department stores. Our mother dressed us so cute. Many people thought we were identical twins. Mama would wash and condition our hair and afterward grease our scalps with Blue Magic, then using a hard, bristled brush, she brushed our curly hair out while creating a smoothly coiled ponytail. Sometimes, mom clothed Denise and me in those beautiful, sky-blue, polyester dresses with the white, chevron patterns across the top. The hem stopped at the bottom of our knees. We completed our attire by wearing white patent leather shoes with ruffled laced socks. I absolutely loved my elegant socks; I tried to wear them with everything. We resembled lovely, bronze-colored, baby dolls. While Mama took excellent care of us, she was saving up enough money to move out of Big Mama's house.

After about four years, she placed a rental deposit on a house in the 900 block of Glen Garden in the Morningside area of Fort Worth, Texas. This was a gigantic milestone, considering we had been living with Big Mama all of our lives. Finally, we were about to move into our "own" residence.

Not too far from Big Mama's house stood a light green home with a large cemented front porch, which set about thirty yards from the street with a gated back-yard sizable enough for two dogs and children to play. I don't really remember packing. I guess our mom packed and had everything delivered without us. Well, that makes sense. Who would have small children assist in the moving process? We probably would have just gotten in the way.

I can still envision my sister and me entering our new home for the first time. The inside was entirely furnished with simple furniture like a sofa, end tables, and bedroom sets for each room, which helped complete the two-bedroom house. Newspaper covered the windows in the back part of the house while curtains were displayed in the living room and Mama's bedroom. Many family members believed Mr. J helped Mama furnish the place. Our mother merely brought clothes and toys. Denise and I shared a room with a full-size bed. The house was heavenly because it belonged to us. Our faces glowed with amazement. The house was perfect; it was like Christmas.

Eventually, we acquired two dogs. Our cousin, Rockie, found a fun-loving little mixed-breed mutt with shaggy brown fur while walking home one day. He didn't know who the dog belonged to, so he immediately named him Poochie. Rockie didn't have a place to keep the puppy; therefore, he gave him to us. We were extremely excited; he was a cute playful little dog. However after a few weeks, we gained another addition. Mr. J, Mama's sugar daddy, brought a larger dog name King to the house. Why was he named King? No one was exactly sure, but some family members believed King was Mr. J's personal dog first; nonetheless, he let us have him because he was looking out for us. Maybe, he thought Poochie wasn't suited for protecting the family, so he gave us the new dog. King was an older, black Lab with bloodshot eyes and a presence that could scare most people. The two canines got along well, so

Mr. J built two dog houses for them. Everything seemed to be all set.

My mom worked diligently to take care of our family, yet it became too much for her to handle. She soon developed a habit that would destroy our happy home.

CHAPTER 3

FAMILY GATHERINGS

WITHOUT a doubt, drinking was a huge part of family gatherings. Uncle Eddie and Aunt Lilly usually walked to the corner store to purchase Coors, except when they were trying to save money. Then, they bought Black Label. This beverage delighted them, but the thought of this intoxicating drink made my sister and me cringe. Nothing good seemed to happen when beer was involved. After Uncle Eddie and Aunt Lilly strolled to the store, they came back with a brown paper bag and some "squares." Next, they presented the case of golden cans with the Coors logo in red, cursive letters. Oh how, I despised the sight of this beverage, but they worshipped this liquid. I could feel their excitement when the cans made their arrival. My relatives' eyes twinkled at the sight of this magical drink. Shortly after Teddy Pendergrass, Kool and the Gang, and The Commodores began to play in the background. The sound of opening beer cans and smoke engulfed the room. The smell of second-hand smoke filled our furniture, clothing, hair, and bodies as usual. We had been exposed to this environment all of our lives. This was our normal. Didn't everybody's house share this aroma? Eventually, Aunt Lilly started her strange type of hoochie coochie dance, which was somewhat embarrassing, at least to us. It reminded me of that painting of people dancing in the show Good Times. As voices bellowed louder and louder, we were told to go to the back room because adults were talking.

Kids weren't allowed to listen to "adult" conversations, so we traveled to the room to play with our dolls while trying to listen without being discovered. We wondered what would happen next because something always happened at these gatherings.

After having a great time drinking, listening to music, and dancing in the living room for hours, then our mother, who was filthy drunk, decided that she would take her festivities to the next level. That meant she was going to get dressed to party at the club called The One Rose. I heard her tell Big Mama, "I'm leaving with Lilly for a few hours. I'll be back."

My grandmother replied, "Okay, Caroline. You hurry back here now." It was apparent from her tone that she didn't want to keep us although she didn't say no. Big Mama was such an enabler.

As my mom struggled to Big Mama's bedroom bumping into walls, she began rummaging through the closet as she joked with her sister. After finding the attire she brought, she took out her black hair pick with the fist on the handle to comb through her Afro. While Mama changed clothes, huge tears welled up in my eyes as I whimpered while peeking and eavesdropping at a distance. However, this didn't seem to faze my mom. She was going anyway. As she staggered toward the door and tried to escape, my whimpering became screams, so I desperately ran to my mother and grabbed her legs. It didn't matter; she rushed out anyway.

My mom started going out to clubs and drinking to relieve stress. I guess this allowed her to escape her pain. She peeled my little hands off of her pants leg and hurried out of the door into the darkness. My sister and I hated The One Rose. We disliked that club because that meant we were going to be separated from our mother.

This was when I realized that alcohol and clubbing were more important than me, so I started rehearsing to myself, *I will never be like my mama. Now, I'm stuck with my grandmother who doesn't particularly like how I came into this world.* My mom couldn't get back soon enough. Staying with my grandmother was complete torture.

CHAPTER 4

BIG MAMA

IRONICALLY, Big Mama wasn't a large woman at all; she was about 5'7" and weighed 115 pounds. Her mahogany skin was flawless, and she wore a Press-n-Curl. She kept her money in a rolled-up napkin inside her bra. She hardly bought anything. I don't know what she was saving for. She was afraid to put her money in the bank because she didn't think it would be safe. I don't remember her working much at all. She was a hypochondriac who always complained about different ailments, but she appeared to be healthy even though she smoked cigarettes like a freight train. She received disability checks while her boyfriend, Mr. Morris, took care of her, but he didn't live with her. He paid her rent and bills. Mr. Morris was an amazing man. He was always thinking about us; he bought us Christmas gifts and made sure Big Mama had enough money to feed us. He was the only grandfather we knew. We heard that Big Mama was married, but her husband abandoned her way before we were born.

I guess she was bitter, so she took it out on others

in her path. She never yelled. She simply used her words in a normal tone, and those words cut like a blade. The daggers made me fearful to hear her voice, so I just merely existed in her presence. Of course, I didn't want to stay with her, but I had no choice. Mama was gone. How could my mom be so careless? Isn't she supposed to protect me?

I was just a child, but I was left worrying about what might happen to her instead. She left walking in the middle of the night, and she was drunk. We didn't live in the best neighborhood. Horrible things were happening daily. Someone could really take advantage of her. Eventually, we fell asleep, and when we woke up the next morning, our mother wasn't back. I continued to rehearse, "I will never be like my mama," and Big Mama kept saying in frustration, "Caroline better get here soon to get these kids. Now y'all get somewhere and sit down." I guess she was concerned about her; however, it seemed like she was more upset about being left to take care of us.

My sister and I played with our baby dolls like usual, but we got into an argument like siblings do. Denise ran into the living room and said, "Shannon took my doll." Big Mama resolved the issue by yelling, "Shannon, get in here!" When I rushed to the living room, she exclaimed, "Shannon, you're a mean, hateful little girl! Give that doll to your sister. That's why we're going to take a trip and stay in a motel, but we're gonna leave you here with your mean self. And that's why you're going to get pregnant before your sister. Give her that doll back!" I didn't know why she was saying this to me. I was only seven. I sheepishly gave my sister the doll and walked away in tears. That statement stuck with me, and I was determined to prove Big Mama wrong.

Everything was always my fault when it came to my grandmother. I could never achieve my sister's status. See, my sister had a different daddy; that made all of the difference in Big Mama's world. I grew up thinking I was mean and nobody liked me because of my interaction with my grandmother.

Every moment, I wondered when my mother would arrive; I was in a prison with Big Mama. This situation would best be described as misery. Several days had passed, and Denise and I didn't know when Mama was coming home. She had to get there soon, or she was going to lose another good job. We wouldn't be able to get our school clothes out of layaway. This was a big deal because we only got new clothes for the start of school, income tax time, and Christmas, but eventually that all disappeared because the money was spent on beer. I thought, *Is she dead? Did someone kill her? Are police going to come to our house and say that they found her body? Will I have to live with Big Mama for the rest of my life?* Minute by minute, we became even more worried.

This was certainly too much for a seven and eight-year-old to handle, but we had no choice. We were given Caroline Ann Baker as a mother, and I just wanted to know why I was being punished with her as a parent. Couldn't God have selected someone more qualified? Someone sophisticated and responsible, a mother who wasn't addicted to a substance. Why did I get her as a mother? Other people seemed to have normal family situations, but I didn't.

While these questions bombarded my mind, I envisioned a white male police officer coming to our door knocking with authority and telling us that they had found her cold limp body in an alley. After all, she did leave walking in the middle of the night, and she could barely stand. I thought I had imagined someone knocking, but to my surprise, it was my mom. She appeared sloppy drunk even after several days. Embarrassed by her state, my sister and I hoped our friends who lived down the street didn't see her stagger up to the door. I guess she had been on a binge for the last few days, but I was relieved to see her—tipsy—but she was alive. At that moment she seemed perfect just because she wasn't dead. After all, she was still my mother.

CHAPTER 5

PLAYING HOOKY FROM SCHOOL

I will absolutely never forget this day. My sister and I woke up. We immediately went to our cubby-sized bathroom and began brushing our teeth. Next, we strolled back to our room to put our dresses on with pants underneath. I hated how Mama made us wear pants with dresses in the winter. She said it would keep us warm, but I just thought we looked ridiculous. I was already embarrassed before stepping foot on the school grounds. Hooray, it's pants with a dress day, I thought, looking like an idiot.

After sulking over my mother's outfit selection, I entered the kitchen and climbed on top of a chair to get the Fruit Loops from the top of the refrigerator. Next, I opened the fridge to get the milk, and we took bowls from the rack that set on the counter close to the faucet. We made our cereal.

Once we were done with breakfast, we put our coats on and prepared to walk out the door to head to school, but Mama stopped us. She instructed, "Go get in the truck." I was puzzled; however, I wasn't going to refuse a ride to school. Aunt Lilly and Mr. BJ were sitting in his tattered dirty green work truck. I thought, *I like rides in the cold, but I don't know if I want anyone to see me get out of this piece of junk.* My sister and I got in first. Then, our mom followed. Mr. BJ instantly said, "Yay for the girls!" with his smoker's laugh. He always seemed excited to see us. He was a joyful and encouraging man even though he was a little shady. My aunt and Mr. BJ were secretly seeing each other. She had a boyfriend at home, and Mr. BJ had once dated Aunt Lilly's younger sister, Aunt Bernice. Even as a little girl, I thought this was wrong, but I wasn't sure because there were a lot of things that didn't make sense in my life. However, I never could have predicted what would happen next. We drove down Glen Garden Street all crammed into this pickup truck. Just imagine five people in the cab of this vehicle. I looked out of the window, and it appeared that we were heading the wrong way. As Mr. BJ continued to drive, the idea of going to school started to fade, and sadness started to take over. It was important that I attend school. This was how I escaped this madness, but now it seemed that we were taking a field trip to some unknown destination. While I glanced out the window, it began to drizzle. This seemed like the longest ride ever. Finally, we made it to an apartment building close to Hemphill Street. I had never been in this area before. Mr. BJ parked the truck, and let us out.

Disappointed, I pulled myself out of the vehicle with dread and dragged my body behind everyone. They would know that I didn't approve of being kidnapped for the day. My sister was excited about missing school, but I was in a state of depression. I wondered, *Why are we randomly visiting Aunt Lilly's apartment? Can't we do this on the weekend? What was I gonna do with no toys, no nothing? Can I just have some paper? Then at least, I can play school.* This was truly a nightmare in the daytime. My education was important, and I needed to be there to learn math, language, spelling, and trace the cursive letter for the day, but instead I was playing hooky, and I didn't know why.

Eventually, we made it upstairs to Aunt Lilly's apartment. When she opened the door, I noticed the efficiency-sized space decorated with Virgin Mary candles all over the place. She had a kitchen and a bedroom, but I don't remember a living room at all. There were colorful Catholic artifacts everywhere. My Aunt Lilly's boyfriend was a Mexican man, who spoke very little English. He was a hard-working man, and he loved Aunt Lilly. He took good care of her. The decorations represented his culture. That was entertaining for a short while.

My sister and I went into Aunt Lilly's bedroom area and sat on her bed near the door. I listened to my mom and aunt talk, but I wanted them to hear my displeasure. I began to moan gradually as well as whimper like a puppy for about fifteen minutes. My mom yelled, "Be quiet before I give you something to cry about!" However, she needed to know that I should have gone to school today, so I ignored her and cried louder. Soon, my crying was heard throughout the whole apartment.

After about two hours of crying, my mother came in the room a little agitated and said, "I told you to close your mouth," so she came toward me with her hand in an upright position and began to spank my bottom. As she spanked me, she said with breaks between each word, "I-told-you-to-shut-up! Now-I'm-going-to-give-you-a-reason-to-cry! When-I-tell-you-to-do-something,-you-better-do-it."

I screamed louder and louder until I didn't have anything left. Finally, I was quiet, but my voice was heard. I fell asleep like I always did after getting a whoopin'. Something inside of me believed things would be better after I woke up.

After about an hour, I opened my eyes and noticed I was in Aunt Lilly's bed, unaware that I had even gone to sleep. Mr. Susana, Aunt Lilly's boyfriend, was home from work by this time. I guess he knew we were there because he bought Denise and me a Pepsi and an Almond Joy candy bar. This was his signature gift for us. Every time we saw him, this is what we received.

We thought the world of Mr. Susana because he always seemed to think about us. My sister said, "Mr. Susana brought you something." She delivered it to me, and I got up to tell him thank you.

While I was drinking the soda and eating the candy bar, my mother came in the room and sat next to me. In a loving voice, she said, "I don't like whoopin' you, so when I tell you to do something, do it so that I don't have to whoop you." She patted me on the back and then left the room.

Shortly after our little talk was over, we gathered our things to prepare to exit the apartment, and we walked down the street looking for Mr. BJ's truck. As it magically appeared, Mr. BJ picked us up and took us home. I still don't know why we went there that day, but I was ecstatic that I never had another day like that again. I accomplished my goal of being heard, so that spanking was worth it.

That year, I missed thirty days because of my mom's random excursions. In spite of it all, I still advanced to the next grade. From that point on, I had perfect attendance. That was also the year I decided I wanted to be a teacher. This way I would never miss school again.

CHAPTER 6

CLASS WITH JIMMY WASHINGTON

OBVIOUSLY missing thirty days of school caught up with me. When I entered third grade the next school year, I had to go to a "special class" on the third floor of D. McRae Elementary and meet with a teacher who helped me with math.

When we were doing an exciting activity, my homeroom teacher always seemed to say, "Shannon and Jimmy! It's time for you to go to resource." I felt like Jim needed this class, but not me because I was smart. They definitely got it wrong. I thought, *Why did my mom sign the paperwork for me to be "special"? She must have gotten it mixed up with gifted and talented. Besides, I had to be gifted since I was proofreading the letters that she sent to school. I capitalized her lowercase "I" that she thought was so cute. I knew it was wrong; the pronoun "I" is capital. I wondered if the teacher noticed that I was correcting her letters. I wished I had confiscated the letter that gave the school staff permission to remove me from my classroom and send me to this dungeon of extra help called resource. They got it all wrong. I only missed thirty days, and it wasn't my fault.*

I hated leaving the outside portable to enter the main building and journey upstairs with Jimmy Washington with his stupid Jheri curl. He seemed happy every time, but I was confident they made a mistake. I knew the teacher felt my resistance because my little personality was so strong. I could simply look and not say a word, and it was as if I just had a full conversation. I thought, *I guess this is what they call filling the gaps.* When a teacher thinks a student is behind, they get additional assistance to progress to the appropriate level. I guess I was one of those kids who needed my gaps filled. After a while, I believed it was okay to get a little assistance. The following year I didn't take any remedial classes. My gaps were filled.

CHAPTER 7

MY BIRTH CERTIFICATE READS FATHER: UNKNOWN

"**DOES** a person have to be married to have kids?" I asked my big sister. She responded, "Yes." Then, I continued, "Well, Mama isn't, and she had us. So, I guess not." As I walked away, I wished Mama had to be married because I would have a daddy. Occasionally, my sister's dad came to visit her and brought her gifts on her birthday. I sat in another room awkwardly moping as my sister lit up like a Christmas tree with enthusiasm. Her dad's name was Jonathan Albert Lusk, but I had no idea who my daddy was.

I wondered, *Where is my father? What does he look like? Do I look like him? Is he tall? Is he light skinned, dark skinned, skinny, or muscular? What kind of person is he? Why doesn't he want me? Is there something wrong with me? Why doesn't my mom make him pay child support? We're struggling, and she won't even request child support. I don't understand.* I was told his nickname is Fat Daddy and that he lives in Royce, Texas. When I do meet him, I am going to beat the crap out of him until I am relieved of all the frustration he has caused me. What type of man has a child and never attempts to take care of him or her? I could only conclude he doesn't care. He is simply a sperm donor, and I wasn't important.

I was told that he came by once when we lived on Glen Garden, and he took my sister to school. He didn't know the difference between Denise and me. My sister was told, "Pretend like you're Shannon, and he's going to take you to school." I remember my sister telling me that he gave her a dollar too. I thought this was a big deal. This angered me; however, my family thought it was funny. I felt like my sister had stolen the only moment I could have had with my father. For a kid who had never met her dad before, this was definitely not a laughing matter. He didn't know my birthday, my favorite color, how old I was, my fears, my life's aspirations, whether I was hungry, if I had clothes, if I were protected, if I were homeless, and he couldn't even identify me in a crowd. Yes, my birth certificate reads unknown because he decided to be just that. He didn't want to inconvenience his life so instead he chose to inconvenience mine. My birth certificate reads Father: UNKNOWN, and he lived up to his name.

CHAPTER 8

THE NIGHT THEY LEFT

O NE Friday evening, Aunt Lilly and Aunt Bernice came over to spend time with my mother. After several hours of drinking, talking, and listening to relaxing music, they decided to go clubbing.

As Mama got dressed, my anxiety level skyrocketed. My nightmare was occurring again. I thought, *Is Denise going to be responsible for us? Are they taking us to Big Mama's house?* It was nighttime, and I was afraid of the dark. The silhouettes on the hallway walls close to our room scared me at night, so my sister walked me to the bathroom in the dark. I was petrified thinking that we might be left alone in the middle of the night. My mom and her sisters chatted while she put on makeup and then combed her hair. I began to cry while shaking nervously. My big sister tried to console me, but I was inconsolable. She rubbed my back and said, "Don't cry, Shannon. We'll be alright." I responded with huge raindrops in my eyes, "Mama's gonna leave us again."

My mom and aunts started to walk toward the door. My seven-year-old body tensed up as I ran in the direction of my mom. I grabbed her, and she pulled my stubby hands off of her and left. The door slammed. Crushed and terrified, I thought, *Why God? Why? What will happen to us during the night?*

My big sister locked the door, and rubbed my back again while drying my tears. I was broken-hearted, but my sister did her best to take care of me. My sister was a tower of strength. She put a blanket over my little quivering body as I lay on the sofa in that gloomy living room. Then, she joined me on the sofa. After a while, we finally fell asleep, but when we woke up our mother wasn't there. I was empty in more ways than one, so we entered the kitchen. Denise jumped on the table like an Olympic gymnast to reach the cereal on top of the refrigerator. Next, I hopped on the counter to grab the bowls. We were efficient at acquiring our tools for breakfast. After collecting the other needed supplies, we poured milk into our bowls of Cap'n Crunch and ate.

Following breakfast, we tried to take our minds off of the obvious by playing with our dolls for hours. We didn't know when she was going to arrive, or if she was going to at all. After a while my sister decided to go across the street to use the phone to call our grandmother. She opened the door, and I watched her cross the street to knock on the neighbor's door. When five minutes passed, she returned. She told me that she talked to Big Mama, but she didn't plan on coming to get us.

I didn't understand how she could allow us to stay alone, and not do anything. *What's wrong with these people?*

Eventually, we ran out of cereal, so we started frying bologna and making sandwiches. We remained in the house because we knew not to go outside. We heard a car drive up outside, and it was our mom's friend, Mr. J. Denise let him in, and we explained everything to him. He told us to keep the door locked and don't let anyone in. Time continued to pass and another day went by, but my mom still didn't show up.

My big sister, who was only eight years old, began to wash our clothes by hand with a bar of soap in the bathtub. I assisted her in washing my clothes. When we were finished, she told me to get the Blue Magic hair grease, a comb from the cabinet, and sit down on the living room floor. She was an excellent stylist of pony-tails and braids, but she wasn't gentle in pulling out the tangles. She smacked me in the head with the comb when she got a little frustrated, but it was worth it. I always looked cute after she finished. Besides, my hair had to be combed before Monday because we had to go to school. I loved school; it was the place where I could escape from my reality for eight hours.

When Monday came, my sister and I got up without an alarm clock and put on our partially dry clothes as well as brushed our teeth. We didn't eat that morning because we had run out of cereal, so we walked to school as we always did. When we arrived at Morningside Elementary, I walked into Mrs. Christian's class. I had made it to my safe place. I wanted to be just like her: amazing. Writing on her chalkboard and teaching the students was my daydream. The day was going well; we had covered reading and math. Now, it was time for writing, my favorite thing to do. I scribbled even when it wasn't time to write.

While having a blast writing cursive letters, my mother walked in, and I thought I was looking at a ghost because she had been gone for so long. I wasn't happy to see her at all. One of my friends asked, "Is that your mother?" I replied, "No, that's my aunt," quietly. I was embarrassed of her. She wasn't drunk; I just felt abandoned. Therefore, I didn't want to claim her as a prize possession when I wasn't hers.

Mrs. Christian said, "Shannon Baker, you're getting an early dismissal." Most kids would have been happy, but not me—I enjoyed school. I didn't want to miss any of it. Walking out of the school and journeying home, I was completely silent. I didn't know what to say, but I wondered, *Where had she been? She hadn't been at the club for this long.* She didn't say anything either; she simply acted like she had been there all along. This was simply the start of even more secrets. Soon, my mom couldn't take care of the household. She lost her job because her clubbing and appetite for alcohol interfered with her ability to work. Eventually, we moved out of our house and had to live with Big Mama. I was thrilled.

CHAPTER 9

MOVING IN WITH BIG MAMA

WITHOUT a doubt, that was the gloomiest day ever. We gathered our items and moved to the Polytechnic area of Fort Worth, Texas. Mr. J packed his green Ford truck with our belongings, and then we traveled to Big Mama's tiny one-bedroom apartment on Avenue E. I believe Mr. J put some of our furniture in his garage.

We settled into the living room, the only space available. I remember placing bags everywhere. We invaded the place. The environment seemed somewhat pleasant at first. Mom slept on the sofa, and we made patlets on the floor in the living room. A "patlet" was simply a blanket with a pillow placed on the carpet. Mama assisted us with laying it on the floor. Then, we performed what became our nightly ritual. Mama placed cotton balls in our ears so that roaches wouldn't get inside as we slept. Daily we made our patlets and placed them in the closet until it was bedtime again. However, I guess we overstayed our welcome.

After living there for a few months, Big Mama decided she was going to move away, and we weren't invited to move with her. This was an awkward situation. For weeks Big Mama packed all of her possessions while we uneasily wondered where we were going to live. That day came; I remember it clearly. My grandmother and Uncle Eddie started placing items on the neighbor's truck. While they picked up things around us, we remained in the empty apartment with nowhere to go. The only items left belonged to us. We sadly looked around. My mother said, "I'm going to turn on the gas, and we're gonna to die because we have no place to go." Horrified, we whimpered as she instructed us, "Lay on the floor." As she turned the knob of the gas valve, she lay down too.

As tears collected in the carpet, I prayed. *God, where are you? Why was I born in this family? I don't understand any of this. Why is she doing this to us? What am I going to do? I'm not prepared to die.* I was an obedient child, so I had to do what Mama said. As we continued to lie on our bellies, Big Mama came back into the apartment and said, "Girl, what are you doing? Get your stuff and come on. I'll let y'all stay a little longer, but you have to find a job."

My mother turned the gas off, and we pitifully put our few boxes on the truck. We were overjoyed that we got to live with Big Mama because we were terrified by our mother's plan. We crammed into the neighbor's truck and headed toward the duplex on Avenue H.

Living with Big Mama was bearable for a while. Some weekends Mr. J came to pick up my mom, and I tagged along. I packed my little bag with enough clothes for the weekend, left with a smile on my face, and a sprint in my step. Denise adored Big Mama, but she wasn't too fond of Mr. J. Therefore, she always stayed with Big Mama and Mr. Morris when we departed.

One day Mr. J made an offer we couldn't refuse. He said we could live with him. I was elated! Finally, we would get our own room again. Also, I welcomed spending every day with Mr. J. That was great because he was like a dad to me. *His fantastic idea answered all of our problems*, I thought. Big Mama was happy too. We couldn't leave fast enough. I wanted to have a family like those on TV.

CHAPTER 10

MR. J

IT'S hard to believe, but Mr. Johnny Green, better known as Mr. J, was simply my mom's sugar daddy. He was in his late fifties or early sixties with mixed gray hair, about six feet tall with dark, chocolate brown skin. He worked hard as a chef at Cook Children's Hospital. He owned a home on Avenue G and had a car along with a nice truck. I enjoyed being with my mom and him to escape Big Mama until he made the generous offer for us to live with him. Maybe, he wanted a family too. Mr. J nicknamed me Suga' Mama, and I loved that name. When we moved to his house, my sister and I shared a room—no more patlets or roaches. I felt like I was living the life, with a mom and dad. However, my sister didn't like Mr. J much because she was the apple of my grandmother's eye. Big Mama despised Mr. J, but he was like the father I never had. He actually cared about me and became an intricate part of my life.

Mr. J used to take my sister and me to church, and, oh, how we enjoyed the heavenly environment. I knew that only God could help me in my situation. The music was delightful; this gospel sound gave me a sense of peace. I remember the choir singing "Don't Wait 'til the Battle Is Over." I found the choir fascinating. I wanted to wear a robe and sing a solo just like the lady who was singing. After attending church, Denise and I started playing church frequently, and I liked being the preacher. I took pleasure in hooping and being the dramatic one. Living with Mr. J definitely made life much better.

Whenever I needed something special at school, he would take pennies from his huge jar of coins and cash them in to purchase items for me. Once I was scheduled to sing in a Christmas program at school, and I wanted him, my mother, and sister to attend. We were required to wear a white blouse and blue skirt, and he made sure I had what I needed. That day, I stayed at school until the program started. When the curtains opened that night, my sister and Mr. J were in attendance, but my mom didn't show up. I was disappointed that she missed this special event; however, I was indebted to Mr. J. No one could ever say anything negative about him because I finally found someone who cared enough to be present in my life.

Except one day, I realized that Mr. J and my mother had been keeping a secret. In the middle of the night, someone started beating on the door viciously, but no one would answer. My mom came to our room and whispered, "Get on the floor, hide, and don't say a word." We had no idea what was happening. I remember having a cold, and I tried to stop coughing. I desperately wanted to be quiet. The lady was yelling, "Open the door!" while she tried to kick the door in. I thought she was going to shoot the house up that night. I could hear glass shattering and her walking toward our bedroom window, but I couldn't stop coughing. She knew we were in the house, and I thought we were going to die that night. However, she traveled back to her vehicle to leave; she had mercy on us.

Maybe it was because we were innocent children, and she had some of her own. The police arrived shortly after she left, and I found out that Mr. J was married. The lady was his wife, and they had been separated for a few years. I was surprised and wasn't sure of what to think. It didn't change what I felt about Mr. J because he could do no wrong in my eyes. After this ordeal, I walked to school the next morning as usual and never said a word. I completed my assignments as if my family life was normal. Again, I could escape my dramatic circumstances with the predictable events of school. I never shared this information with anyone; I didn't think anyone else was experiencing situations such as this. Besides, I had become a master of keeping a secret, which made me quiet and shy.

Eventually, my mom started going out clubbing without Mr. J, and she began seeing another man,

Lawrence. He would come and pick up my mom from Mr. J's house. They would sit outside in his car. Even as a small child, I thought this was disrespectful. Soon my mom wasn't coming home at all.

At this time my Uncle Cary and new girlfriend took the opportunity to move into Mr. J's house, and he was bad news. He was known for drug abuse, robbery, and violence, and his girlfriend, Tiny's profession was prostitution. He planned to put her on the streets to make money. I knew nothing good would come from this. My sister and I heard our family saying that she had AIDS, but we didn't care. She was actually spending time with us. Tiny taught Denise and me how to play different card games. We had a blast with her.

Occasionally, we saw our mom. She began living with Lawrence. This was when we felt she picked a man over her children. We knew we weren't her priority. Finally, Mr. J packed our bags and took us over to our grandmother's house to live. I was extremely devastated. I thought, *How could he drop me off with Big Mama, the woman who hated me?* Eventually, I forgave him because I realized I really wasn't his responsibility.

While living on the south side of Fort Worth, I continued to be concerned about Mr. J because I heard that Uncle Cary had taken over his home and started selling his belongings to get drugs. It was no longer the serene home that I remembered. A few months later, I learned that Mr. J had a heart attack while driving. He drove into a tree and died. I blamed Uncle Cary for placing him in this stressful situation. He was the only person I could count on, and now he was gone. His funeral was scheduled to take place in Terrell, Texas. I wasn't able to attend because none of my available family members had a car, nor could they drive. Distraught, I cried in private and isolated myself. I kept a lot inside. After all, I had been trained to keep secrets. I shared my concerns with God, but I felt like he wasn't listening. Besides, why did he put me in this family?

CHAPTER 11

UNCLE CARY

WHEN I think of Uncle Cary, I don't have any positive thoughts; actually my stomach hurts. My earliest memory of him was when we traveled to see him in a small town in Texas. They used to say he was on a vacation, so my interest was piqued when Aunt Bernice, Big Mama, and Uncle Eddie mentioned we were going to visit him.

I recall piling into Aunt Bernice's car like sardines and making the journey to this exotic place, Huntsville. Well maybe, it wasn't exotic, but my Aunt Bernice was dressed so fancy I thought it had to be special. She always looked captivating; she wore a peach colored chiffon jump suit. As she walked, she resembled a beautiful *Ebony* magazine model. The only problem was we had just arrived at the Texas State Penitentiary at Huntsville.

Overwhelmed by the elaborate fence surrounding the place, I scanned the location. There were armed guards in a tower that was positioned in the middle of the yard. They appeared to be ready for combat at any time. Fear took over my little body as we walked to the entrance and waited with the others who hoped to see their loved ones. When it was time to enter, a man dressed in a brown uniform strolled out with authority and gave us some instructions. As we were walking down this long sidewalk to reach the main building, I began to wonder if children should be allowed here.

Approaching the door, a loud unlocking sound was made. After everyone entered, I heard that loud locking sound again. Immediately, I knew I never wanted to come to this place again. This wasn't a good place to be. I'm not sure of what Uncle Cary did because Big Mama always said he was innocent.

We went to the visitors' area, and then we were told that only three people at a time could enter to see him. First, my grandmother and aunt went to a special room to visit with him while Uncle Eddie watched us. We purchased snacks from the vending machine while waiting. Sitting in the waiting chamber eased our worries for a moment, but we were still aware that we weren't at a carnival. Aunt Bernice came out to get Uncle Eddie while Big Mama remained. She stayed with us for about fifteen minutes, and then she exchanged places with Uncle Eddie and Big Mama. Finally, it was our time to go.

In great anticipation, we nervously strolled to the area, and saw our uncle sitting there behind a glass window in a white outfit with a smile on his face. I believe he was in his early twenties, but his dark brown skin looked hard, and his demeanor was tough, even though he beamed with delight. I recall him asking about how we were doing in school, but the rest is a complete blur. He was glad to see us, but I wasn't too sure about seeing him. Something about this whole situation shaped what I thought of him. If he had to be caged up like an animal, he must have done something extremely bad. I couldn't wait to get out of that place. I guess you can say I was "scared straight". I would never be found in a place like this again. I learned a valuable lesson that day.

Months later, Uncle Cary was released. It was a joyous occasion when he came home. He celebrated by bringing his son to visit the family. We were all excited to see him. We hadn't met his son before because he had been on "vacation". My uncles and aunts gathered at Big Mama's to welcome our new addition. The excitement could be felt in the air. Everyone smiled, and the beer had already been purchased.

When he arrived, we all hugged him and Lil' Curtis. It was a beautiful day, so Uncle Cary told Curtis, Denise, and me to go outside to play. After we had been playing "Cowboys and Indians" for a while, Uncle Cary interrupted us without any warning. He grabbed Lil' Curtis angrily by the arm because he thought we were mistreating his son. It was extremely bizarre. He growled, "I'm gon' come back tonight to kill all of y'all for treating my son like that!" When Uncle Cary made a promise, we knew he was going to carry it out. I thought, *I'm not sure why he thinks we would hurt our cousin. We were glad to see him.* Beside, we were docile children.

As he collected their items, Big Mama pleaded with him, "Cary don't go." Driven by anger, he hurried out of the door walking while holding Curtis. The rest of the evening we remained at home in fear. This puzzled me, but everyone continued to chat and tried to return to normalcy. Meanwhile, my aunts and uncles left, but I kept hearing Uncle Cary's statement in my head until I heard the screeching sound of a car pull up in the driveway. Next, we heard an erratic knock at the door. We didn't know what he had in store, so we quietly departed out of the back door into the darkness. We had to move swiftly before he realized we were in the backyard. Uncontrollably my heart skipped beats, and I felt like I was going to throw up. I thought, *Is this how I'm going to die?* As we traveled through the lawn brushing up against tree branches, we made it into the alleyway and escaped his demonic plot. Uncle Cary was a heroin addict; he struggled with addiction for years. I remember him pushing his own mother down a flight of stairs because he wanted money to get a fix. I was grateful that he didn't locate us that night at a neighbor's house.

The next time I had an episode with Uncle Cary was

when we lived on Hattie Street. We were simply relaxing one weekend, hanging around the house. Uncle Cary got up from the sofa and opened the refrigerator and said, "Who ate my sardines?" No one replied, so he began to rant. "I'll tell you what. I'm gonna kill whoever ate my sardines. I'm gonna come back and kill all of y'all tonight since no one knows who did it." He started to get dressed and terror filled the tiny apartment as he prepared to leave. I don't know who ate the sardines, but I was thinking, *Please give them back!* Again, we stayed at home and pretended like it was a regular day.

That night we couldn't go to sleep. As we tossed and turned, suddenly we heard someone revving his or her engine outside, and we peeked out to see Uncle Cary. He knocked at the door while cursing at the top of his lungs. We listened to him from the other side of the door; I knew that we were going to die. My grandmother came from her bedroom and picked up the only weapon available, a skillet, to hit him with if he forced himself inside. He moved from knocking on the door to the window, and he began breaking the glass. When he stuck his head inside to climb in, my grandmother whacked him on the head several times with the skillet. By this time, we could hear the police sirens, and we felt relieved.

Uncle Cary escaped with bumps and bruises on his head after realizing the police weren't far away. Uncle Eddie escaped out of the back window of the apartment while Uncle Cary was wracking havoc at the door and called the police from someone's house.

I learned a very valuable lesson about drugs from Uncle Cary. He was a different person when he wasn't in control of his mental capacity. The idea of not being able to manage my mind wasn't something I ever desired. Therefore, I was never interested in alcohol or drugs; I knew the results first hand. Uncle Cary represented the ultimate embarrassment, and I didn't want anyone to know I was related to him. I thought I might see his mug shot on the news one day for doing something extremely shameful, but before that happened he was sentenced to life in prison. I never saw him again. He had been in and out of prison so many times; the previous judge told him if he returned he was staying for life. He robbed an elderly man and had to spend the rest of his life in prison. What a miserable life. I was ashamed that he was a part of my family. He made me feel worthless because I was one of his relatives. I was afraid that we had the same DNA, so I might turn out like him. I am glad this was just an awful thought and not a fact. Being a criminal isn't innate.

CHAPTER 12

COONIE AND TINA

AFTER being dropped off at Big Mama's, we began to settle into our new home. We made friends with kids in the community when we went outside to play at the neighborhood park. While on the swings, we were introduced to Coonie and Tina, who lived in the apartment complex down the street. They resided with their mom and stepfather, the model family in my eyes. Ms. Griffin cooked every day, and their house was always immaculate. Their stepdad, Felton, had a truck and a job. This was almost unheard of in our community. They even went to church.

Well, one evening I ran down the street to recruit someone to play with, and I met Tina. She was a light-skinned freckle-faced African-American girl with a huge smile. As I sprinted, I saw Tina wearing a T-shirt covered with cake icing. I asked, "What happened?" With enthusiasm she replied, "We had a carnival at church! And we had a cakewalk! I won an entire cake!"

I responded, "I want to go to your church." I thought, *I want some cake too!*

That evening I went home and asked my grandmother if we could go to church. Of course, I needed my sister to go with me because we did everything together. She said, "Yes." Big Mama wouldn't dare tell us we couldn't go to church. Most black people have an appreciation for God even if they don't attend church. Grateful that she said yes, I began to prepare for church. I ironed my clothes and laid everything out. I knew they were going to have a cakewalk during the Sunday morning service. My sister and I went to sleep anxiously thinking about church the following day.

We woke up bright and early for a Sunday and strolled down the street to Coonie and Tina's house. We knocked on the door. They were waiting on us, so we immediately started walking toward the church. I was a little surprised we were walking, but it didn't matter. We were on our way to get cake. We sauntered up the sidewalks of Hattie Street and turned on Bessie Street. It was about a fifteen-minute walk, then we arrived. We hiked up the steps and opened the doors. When we entered, I saw red carpet and wooden pews covered with red cloth. At that moment, I knew I was in the right place. The people came to greet us. They seemed like angels because their spirits were so sweet. We sat down and got ready for the service. Church began with inspirational music; it reminded me of the music I heard when we went to church on Easter. It was soothing and gave me a sense of hope like no other music. This place was magical.

A man who looked like Mr. J was the pastor of the church. He came to the podium and preached a sermon. I don't really remember the message, but I knew I wanted to be a part of this. I had forgotten about the cake, and I was eager to attend the next service. Afterward, I felt like I had found hope and love for the first time. That week, I thought about my experience, so I decided to join the next Sunday. The people were exceptionally kind; it almost seemed unreal. I realized I needed whatever they had.

The following Sunday Pastor Caver preached, and before the usher could put the chair out, I briskly walked down the long aisle of red carpet desperate to be rescued and sat in the pastor's large throne-like seat. I wasn't going to miss this opportunity. They couldn't get the chairs out fast enough. The pastor laughed; he thought it was cute how I rushed down. I knew I wanted to accept Jesus into my heart; I needed him urgently. He kindly showed me to the chairs in front of the pulpit as the ushers brought them to the front. As I moved to the seat, I could hear "O Happy Day" by Edwin Hawkins resounding in my ears:

O Happy Day . . .

O Happy Day. . . .

When Jesus washed,

He washed my sins away,

He taught me how to watch fight and pray,

He taught me how to live rejoicing every day,

As I sat down, the pastor came from the pulpit with the microphone. He said, "Hello, young lady," in his distinguished preacher voice. Next, he asked, "What's your name?"

"Shannon Baker," I said.

Pastor Caver continued, "Do you want to accept Jesus Christ into your heart today?"

I responded, "Yes, sir."

Then, he stated, "I have a few questions I need to ask you." I nodded and thought, *I hope I can answer these questions.*

He asked, "Do you believe that Jesus Christ died on the cross for you?"

I replied, "Yes."

He continued, "And rose on the third day?"

I said, "Yes."

Then, he quoted the New International Version of Romans 10:9, "'If you declare with your mouth, Jesus is Lord and believe with your heart that God raised him from the dead, you will be saved.' It's that easy. You are saved. The angels in heaven are rejoicing because you accepted Christ today. Now, church members, please come around and welcome Shannon into the family of God."

I thought, *For the first time, I finally did something right.* Filled with excitement, I welcomed the idea of being in God's family, especially since mine wasn't perfect. I remember feeling like I was Jesus' baby sister. Little did I know how my relationship with God would carry me through some dark days.

CHAPTER 13

GOD'S LOVE

I'M glad God found me. That cakewalk was a powerful thing in my life. From that point on, my sister and I attended church like it was our extra-curricular activity. Church truly kept us out of trouble, especially in our teenage years. We didn't miss any church revivals, Wednesday night Bible studies, choir rehearsals, youth, or BTU meetings. Church was like a Bible institute for us because we learned so much about the word. The youth was assigned a monthly memory scripture, and we could win a prize if we recited the scripture. I learned them all. The first one was to the tune of "Row Row Row Your Boat" so I sang, "Second Timothy 2:15 this is what it says. Second Timothy 2:15 this is what it says. Study to show thyself approved unto God a workman not needed to be ashamed rightly dividing the word of truth." I loved learning the word of God. This is what gave me hope while I wasn't at church. I made some mistakes because I was trying to live a lifestyle so different than my environment.

After a while, I actually started teaching Sunday

school for the little children. My sister and I ushered and sang in the choir. We also became the church custodians. Pastor Caver made sure we had a little change in our pockets; we also paid tithes from our earnings. We knew what the Bible said about money.

After joining World Missionary Baptist Church, we acquired a support system, especially in the Caver family. Clara Caver played the role of a competent mother, and she did it well. She invited us to her house so that she could wash our dirty coats. We weren't always the cleanest little girls. I also recall her coming to our apartment to pick us up to take us shopping.

One winter, I remember the only pair of shoes I had was a pair of reddish colored jellies with the crisscross pattern that we bought from Motts. I wore those plastic shoes with socks in the cold and rain. I knew I needed some closed-toe shoes, but I didn't know when I was going to get any. No one in my family seemed to be concerned that I didn't have the proper shoes to wear during the winter season except Sister Caver. One day she came and picked us up and took us to Payless to get new shoes. She told us that we could get whatever we wanted. I had the biggest smile plastered on my face. At that moment, I knew that God loved me because he was constantly showing his love through the Caver family.

Also, I will never forget the day that Sister Caver came to William James Middle School to check on me.

I was sitting in class, and the teacher said, "Shannon Baker, you have a visitor." To my surprise, it was Sister Caver. She looked more beautiful than ever because she was there just to see me. I cheerfully walked outside the classroom to talk to her. I forget what we discussed. I just wished she was my mom. She was better equipped. If I were an employer, I would have told her that she had been selected for the position that day.

Pastor Caver filled the void of Mr. J. Immediately after his death, I started attending church. Pastor Caver's stature, complexion, compassion, and size all resembled Mr. J; however, he was extremely intelligent, whereas Mr. J couldn't read, but that didn't bother me because he loved me. Pastor Caver had a great job working for the Federal Aviation Administration. With his salary, Sister Caver was a stay-at-home mom, and he funded the church while supporting his family. I found that to be pretty amazing.

I thought the Cavers were a family of geniuses. Pastor and Sister Caver were exceptionally bright as well as their son and daughter. Michelle and Dimitri attended Dunbar Magnet High School. Michelle wanted to become a teacher and so did I; therefore, I watched her every move. I don't think she was aware of it. I even tried to write like her; she had beautiful cursive penmanship. Dimitri was a prodigy on the piano and organ. I was intrigued by his ability to play at such a young age.

He learned to play by ear when he was in the seventh grade, and his skills were impressive. He allowed me to follow him around as if I were his little sister. He even introduced me as such.

Eventually, they began including us in holidays and family trips. They came and picked us up for Thanksgiving and Christmas. There were many holidays that we wouldn't have had a traditional Thanksgiving or Christmas meal, but the Cavers ensured that we did. The family bought us gifts like we were truly their own. I was fascinated by their generosity. Sister Caver always made receiving gifts entertaining. Once she created a scavenger hunt for us to find our gifts. We all had a blast running around discovering presents. Being with the Cavers allowed us to be normal kids.

Eventually, I began to ask God, "Why aren't the Cavers our parents? I told God constantly I wanted the Cavers as parents, but he didn't seem to be listening for years. We received special treatment from the Cavers. I believe the other members noticed it, but they wouldn't dare say a word. However, it was apparent. Whenever we moved, the Cavers traveled wherever we were and picked us up for all of the events. At the time, I don't think we really understood the sacrifices they made for us, or maybe we did and this is why we wanted them as parents. If they could care about us without being our parents, we would have no worries as their children.

They took more interest in us than our biological family. It was obvious that they loved us.

CHAPTER 14

ABANDONED

WHAT was supposed to be a short time became days, months, and years. My grandmother had been keeping us for some time with no assistance from my mom. My mother was enjoying her life with her boyfriend, Lawrence, who lived on the other side of Fort Worth. I couldn't believe she would leave me with Big Mama, who hated me. Every time she had an opportunity to tear me down, she did with no hesitation. The only thing that kept me sane was going to church and school. I treasured both of those places because being there meant I didn't have to be in that dark, depressing apartment. I tried to get encouragement wherever I could. I tried hard in school because I could get awards that validated my belief that I was intelligent. The people at church actually knew I existed and gave me attention. However, when I made it home, I was reminded of who I was and what I was: abandoned! My mother selected a man over us. One day I remember picking up the phone and dialing my mother's boyfriend's number. I had planned on telling her exactly what I thought. At the age of eleven, I was certain of my feelings, and my mother needed to know. The phone rang. Rrring . . . rring . . . ring . . . Someone picked up the phone, and I said, "Can I speak to my mother, Caroline?"

The person on the other end said, "Let me go get her."

Then, I heard, "Hello." With all the emotion I could muster, I shouted, "I hate you!" in a convincing tone and hung up the phone. I went to the only bedroom to think about what I had done. She called back. Really, she actually called. She tried to console me. Well, it didn't matter. The damage had been done. It was the truth; I really hated her. I felt like I should feel guilty for saying that to my mom. After all, the Bible says I'm supposed to respect her, but I didn't. I believed she needed to know, and I wouldn't take it back. From that point on, my mom somewhat tiptoed around me because she didn't know what I was capable of saying. I just might tell her the truth.

Eventually, Big Mama got tired of taking care of us, especially following a visit from Pastor Caver. Denise went to Bible study extremely upset one day. She sat there in silence, which wasn't typically her behavior. Therefore, everyone knew something was wrong with her. Pastor Caver invited her into his office, so he could question her discreetly. She reluctantly told him about an incident that occurred with one of our uncles. Uncle

Peter got angry with her for some reason and threw an object at her, so she was afraid to go home. The next day Pastor Caver showed up to investigate the situation. Big Mama and Uncle Peter acted kind while he was there, but they talked about him when he left. Big Mama even got on the phone and started calling others to complain about his actions. It hurt my heart that they would say such awful things about him. He didn't deserve that; he was simply trying to protect us. My sister and I were thankful that he stood up for us. However, I believe this pushed Big Mama over the edge, so she packed our things in preparation of dropping us off with our mom at Lawrence's house.

CHAPTER 15

LAWRENCE'S HOUSE

I will never forget that morning. Aunt Bernice arrived, and we placed our things in her car. She drove while Big Mama sat in the passenger seat as we nervously reclined in the back with our black trash bags filled with our possessions. When we approached the duplex, I began to feel anger, uncertainty, and anticipation. My sister and I walked to the porch of Lawrence's house with all of our bags. My grandmother didn't get out. My aunt pressed the gas when our mother answered the door of the predominantly white wood-framed house trimmed in black, and they were gone.

Apprehensively, we walked into the dark, cluttered one-bedroom place. Our mom told us to put our belongings in their bedroom. Lawrence was at his mom's house down the street. We wondered how he was going to receive us. Settling into our new place, we put our things into the dresser drawers. We explored the house and discovered there was no television. This was a huge problem because we were older, so we no longer played with dolls. I was an eighth grader attending William

James Middle School, and Denise was a sophomore at Green B. Trimble Technical High School. We wondered what we were going to do for entertainment. My mom stayed with us for a while. Then, she journeyed down the street to join the mystery man. We remained in our new house until it was dark. Finally, we heard our mom and Lawrence arrive. Eager to meet the man who stole our mother, we were intrigued. He had to be something special. While waiting in the back room, we overheard curse words filling the air along with what sounded like a scuffle. It seemed that our mom was being attacked, so in protection mode, we ran out of the room and found him choking her. Immediately, we ran to her defense and began punching and kicking him. Our mom yelled, "Stop! Get off of him!" She was upset with us. I couldn't believe it. We went back to the room while discussing the fiasco wondering, *What have we gotten ourselves into?* Powerless, we had nowhere else to go. This was our first day, and it foreshadowed what was to come. For the next few days, we stayed in the house, miserable because there wasn't anything to do.

Eventually, we began going to Mrs. Kiel's, Lawrence's mother's house, as well. She was a sweet lady and an amazing cook. She worked hard to provide for her forty-year old son. Lawrence went to his parents' house around seven in the morning. He would begin his routine by sitting on the right side of the cream sofa embellished with brown flowers. When he wasn't relaxing there, an indentation of his butt was carved into the cushion. At noon, he walked to the liquor store along with his two dogs and purchased his favorite beverage. After returning to his mother's house, he sat on the sofa and drank several bottles of vodka and began to rant as usual. I realized his problem was worse than my mother's. I wondered how he had become such a worthless drunk. One day, my mom mentioned the situation that changed his life. He was partying at a club on Rosedale Street. A man doused him with gasoline and set him on fire. She explained that he was screaming while running around trying to put the fire out. Because of this incident, his caramel brown skin was shriveled up, especially the left side of his body. His hair wouldn't grow in certain areas of his head. I believe he tried to cope with his condition by drinking.

My sister and I couldn't tolerate him because he was a loud abusive drunk. Often he yelled at us while our mom was at work. However, one day we had enough. While we were passing through the living room, he said, "Get out of here and the horse you rode in on!" He rushed toward us with his fist balled up while trying to balance his feet. He continued, "I'll knock your big 'strang' loose!" I quickly looked at a mirror on the end of a coffee table and broke it in an effort to slice him up. As I lifted the mirror piece, I heard God clearly say,

"Don't!" I hesitated and stopped. Then, we left, but my sister devised a plan. We went to our home. My sister was furious, so she plotted to kill Lawrence that night. Denise really wasn't violent, but she never liked any of my mother's boyfriends. He was truly the worst. I recall her grabbing a moderate sized knife from the kitchen and saying, "I'm going to use this knife, and I'm going to kill him tonight." We were sick of Lawrence. I was going along with the plan. Besides, I always followed my big sister's lead.

That evening, the Cavers picked us up for the revival. When we got to church, we ushered and sang in the choir as usual. Pastor Caver preached, but this time he had a word of knowledge. This meant God gave him a special word for someone, and it was urgent. He said, "I see a knife with a black handle. I believe someone is planning to use this knife. Don't do it. This is your warning." We knew he was talking about us, so we listened because we knew that message was coming straight from God. Only God could know our plan. After that, we simply tried to stay out of Lawrence's way. We knew he was crazy, but that was who our mom selected, and we couldn't do anything about it.

CHAPTER 16

THE NIGHT I'LL NEVER FORGET

MRS. Keil went out of town to visit her mom in Kaufman, Texas. I believe Lawrence had just left. I'm sure he staggered to his friend's house while his dog followed him down the street, so he was around the corner hanging out with some friends. My mom was sitting in the living room drinking some beer. Denise and I were in the back room of Mrs. Keil's house. We had been staying there temporarily since the electricity and water were turned off at Lawrence's house.

We were alone with our mother, and this almost never happened. Someone was always there. All of a sudden our mom's voice echoed, "Come here, Denise and Shannon!" Not eager to go, we sluggishly moved her way. We obediently showed up at her side in the living room. When we got there, she was sitting on Lawrence's sofa. She said in a slurred tone, "Sit on my lap." This was completely awkward because she didn't show much affection when she was sober, but now she wanted to hug us and tell us how much she loved us. I didn't like how this felt at all, but we went along with it. She hugged us as she said, "I love y'all," and she kissed us. Following these actions, she walked to the kitchen and grabbed the largest butcher knife she could find then began to come after us. Confused by what was happening, Denise swiftly ran to the side door of the kitchen and headed outside, and my mom followed her with the knife. I entered Mrs. Keil's bedroom and hid in the closet. While I was in the closet smelling the stench of feet from the shoes, I cried and asked God, "Why was I born in this family?" I was learning all of these wonderful Bible stories and scriptures at church about how I was supposed to live as a Christian. I had been praying and asking questions all of my life. I was wondering, *Why is this happening to me. Are these scriptures a joke? Is help really on the way?Everybody else has normal families. But, why did I get this? Why? Why? Why . . . was this mother you gave me going to come and find me in the closet and kill me?*

While I was questioning God, I heard the door. *Who is it?* I thought. I didn't say a word, and I wasn't coming out. Was she back to complete the job? Then, I heard, "Shannon! Shannon! Shannon!" It was my sister's voice, so I came out.

As I looked at her, I didn't see any stab wounds; therefore, I asked, "Where is she?"

She replied, "She's still out there. Let's go before she gets back," she continued.

I remember walking out into the darkness while looking down the street for a figure with a knife, but we didn't see anyone. We decided to use our track skills to sprint down the small hill of Mrs. Keil's house and head around the corner to our aunt's house.

When we arrived on Aunt Jeraline's porch, we knocked vigorously until someone answered. We asked to use the phone, and we called Sister Caver to tell her the story. We didn't even bother telling our aunt since her boyfriend was just as irrational as Lawrence. After we shared the tale with Sister Caver, she said she was going to come and pick us up. Within about thirty minutes, Sister Caver was there in that maroon Toyota Corolla. I was extremely ecstatic to see her, but I was still in a fog about the entire situation. I don't remember saying much because we were embarrassed. We couldn't understand why the woman who was supposed to love us would kiss us, hug us, and then try to kill us. I will never understand that.

The next day she didn't even remember what happened; it was all a blur. However, it shaped my life forever. I was puzzled for days. I said, " Lord, I just want my mother to be just that, a mother. Her actions don't fit the characteristics of what I think a mother should be. Why is that so hard for her? We are good kids. We very seldom get into any trouble. We make A's and B's in school, and we are always at church. We desperately want her to love us, but she doesn't."

We knew our place was somewhere after alcohol, Lawrence, and clubbing. The one time that I knew she loved me was when she carried me for nine months because she could have aborted me, so I'll take it. She gave me life.

CHAPTER 17

LIFE AFTER THE ORDEAL

WHEN Sister Caver picked us up, Pastor Caver was out of town. Michelle and Dimitri were away at college, so neither one of them was home. We arrived at their beautiful home in Stop Six, and Sister Caver opened the black iron door. We walked inside, and she told us to go into Michelle's old room. There were two twin beds in there. She gave us some t-shirts to sleep in because we didn't bring any clothes. My sister and I got into the bed. We fell fast asleep since we knew we were safe.

The next morning my sister and I chatted about going back. We were a little worried, but we knew we had to return. We eventually got out of bed and went to the bathroom to wash our faces and brush our teeth. We smelled the aroma of bacon cooking, so we headed to the kitchen. By this time, Pastor Caver was back. We immediately said hello to him. We sat down as Sister Caver fixed our plates. I thought, *This is what a mother is supposed to do. Why weren't we born in this family?* She brought our plates over with bacon, eggs, and toast.

She asked if we wanted jelly for our toast, and I replied, "Yes, please."

While we ate, my sister shared what happened that evening by simply saying, "She hugged us and kissed us. Then she entered the kitchen, grabbed a knife and attempted to kill us." Pastor and Sister Caver responded, "We wanted to adopt y'all when you first came to the church. You can live with us." As I listened in silence, Sister Caver said, "I will take you to your house to collect your items, so that you have all of your belongings. I wondered, *How will Mama react when we arrive to get our things? Will she fight to keep us? She isn't going to let them just take us. Is she?*

After breakfast, we drove to the white and blue house on Belzise Terrace, Mrs. Keil's house, and the Cavers parked the World Missionary Baptist Church van with signs plastered on both sides in the driveway. My sister and I quickly jumped out, rushed inside, and located several large black trash bags in the kitchen. Lawrence was sitting in his regular spot on the sofa drinking vodka, and Mama lay on the love seat while *The Price Is Right* played in the background. We proceeded to collect our items. No one tried to stop us. We emptied all the things from our dresser drawers as well as the closet. Next, we hopped back into the large vehicle, and no one tried to stop us. No one even asked us where we were going or where we had been. My mom didn't even try to fight the Cavers about trying to take us. She simply lay on the living room sofa with a hangover and never moved. I thought, *Get up! Run to the car door and yell at them! Don't let them take us without a fight!* I envisioned my mom running outside screaming at the top of her lungs, "You ain't gon' take my #@$ kids!" But, she did nothing. There was complete silence, and no one moved or spoke. We left without a struggle, and I was left to draw my own conclusions. Maybe she was happy we were finally out of her hair, and she could live her life with her man, Lawrence. Once again, I knew I wasn't on her list of important things. I didn't make the cut. I wanted the Cavers to be my parents, but I didn't imagine it would happen this way. God had finally answered my prayers, and there was proof that he was hearing me. I had mixed emotions, but I knew this was the best move for us.

I worried about what the Cavers would tell the church because they would notice that we were staying in their house since we were holding church at the Cavers' home while the new church was being built. We tried to brace ourselves for the embarrassment, but it was unavoidable.

CHAPTER 18

MY BIG SISTER

EVER since I could remember, my big sister took care of me. She was like my second mother because she actually looked after me more than my mama. I adored my sister. We were about the same height (under 5 feet), but she was considered the skinny one. When we were younger, she wore a six slim while I wore a six regular. She maintained her slender figure while I was considered the thick one. She started wearing a Jheri curl when she was in the fifth grade. Uncle Lee, who was a hairstylist, fixed her hair and cut it into a sassy new do, so she was pretty trendy. As she got older, she changed to a perm, and it was cut in a cute style that everyone was wearing. Denise Renee Baker was a diva.

She was extremely loquacious, so she talked for me. I could be as quiet and shy as I wanted to be because my sister was my translator. She was a talented athlete. She played basketball and ran track. She was an excellent sprinter. She did all of the latest dance moves; I idolized her. My sister could do everything; there wasn't anything that I thought she couldn't do. We had a bond that no one could break because she was the only family member I could count on. Besides that, we had almost died several times together. I can't say that I had these experiences with anyone else. We fought and argued like most siblings, but nobody could stand between my sister and me.

When we moved to the Cavers, it was her senior year. As the weeks passed, I became increasingly concerned. We were getting accustomed to being a part of the Caver family and having our needs met. This was a new situation. The Cavers made sure that she took senior pictures and prepared for college. As time got closer for her to attend college, I became extremely depressed, but I was proud of my big sister. She was going to Prairie View A & M University, which was where the sophisticated black people attended school. She dreamed of becoming an accountant because she was exceptionally good with numbers. As time drew near, I appeared to be sad, but inside I wanted her to do well. I needed someone in my family to be a success. No one in our family had graduated from high school or attended college, and most of the women couldn't drive a car. She had already exceeded the expectations. I wanted her to soar like an eagle.

The last week before she had to leave, she purchased a small stuffed animal, and she gave it to me and said, "When you're sad just hold this stuffed animal and think of me." She had never left me alone. All of the events that we had been through quickly flashed through my mind, and I was completely drained. What was I going to do without my big sister! That week ended rapidly, and we had to drive her to a small city outside of Houston, Texas. I remember seeing prairie dogs on the lawn. I hadn't seen those creatures before. Eventually, we found her dorm. We took her things up a long flight of stairs because the elevators weren't working. Pastor Caver, Sister Caver, and I placed her things in the room swiftly and left. Tears rolled down my cheeks. My emotions were mixed. A little upset, I wondered, *Why did we leave so quickly?* Later I learned they didn't want to cry and create a huge scene. I recalled thinking, *Who's going to talk for me? I'm so afraid. I don't have any friends. Who will I hang out with at school? I've always hung out with my sister and her friends. I knew she got tired of me, but now, I'm alone.* I was extremely quiet on the way back, and for the next couple of weeks, I was in a daze.

I remember someone at church asking, "Do you miss your sister?" I immediately burst out crying and ran to the restroom. They didn't realize it was like asking me whether I missed my mother. She protected, fed, comforted, supported, listened, and taught me. They didn't realize she wasn't just my sister. She was my mother and best friend. I could share everything and anything with her. She was the only one on the planet that I could do that with because I didn't trust anyone else.

CHAPTER 19

FINDING HER PURPOSE

IT took a few months for me to adjust to living with the Cavers by myself, but I liked having my own room and a stable family. I was a junior in high school at this time, and I hadn't seen my mom since the day we left. I learned to deal with difficult situations by blocking them out of my mind. I remember my sister going to counseling, but I didn't feel like I needed it.

I was doing fine. I performed well in school and had no interest in boys because I believed boys would simply get in the way of my dreams, and no little knucklehead deserved the privilege of altering my future. Besides, I had been taught well by Pastor Caver. I attended "What God Says about Sex" seminars for six years. I knew how to respond to a little boy who only wanted one thing. I wasn't at all fascinated by babies. I didn't want anyone to see me holding a baby even if he or she were my baby cousins. No one would think a child belonged to me. I had seen it time and time again. Many young ladies in my community were having babies, and I refused to be in that number. I took a great deal of pride in being different. I wouldn't entertain the conversation of a young man who seemed "too smooth". I could discern him a mile away, and he wouldn't have a chance with me no matter how cute he was. Besides, I had to prove that Big Mama was wrong about me. Her statement was engraved in my mind.

That year something remarkable happened. I always had a close relationship with my English teachers. It started in middle school with Mrs. Wolanski and Mrs. Brownlee. They were incredible educators. However, my English teachers in ninth and tenth grades were mediocre, but my eleventh grade year was different. I walked into class and sat in the back, hoping not to be noticed. Then, this man in his early thirties wearing a plaid, button-down collared shirt with khaki pants appeared in front of the class at his wooden podium. He seemed serious about his position. He explained that he graduated from Yale. I looked up attentively; I was elated that a teacher of that quality would teach at my school. I thought, *I'm going to learn everything I can from this man. I will be a sponge.* I loved English; the patterns and rules of grammar were easy for me.

Whenever Mr. Henry returned graded papers, he always praised me in front of the class. He didn't know how much I needed that. My peers thought of me as the teacher's pet, and I enjoyed it. I understood that Mr. Henry was a genius; others didn't quite get him. I remember him typing his infractions on a typewriter before technology was introduced to the classroom. I felt extremely blessed to have him as a teacher.

So one day I invited Pastor Caver to meet him after school. Mr. Henry was truly overjoyed to encounter Pastor Caver, "Shannon's father". After a while, we began calling Pastor and Sister Caver Mom and Dad because it was easier than trying to explain the situation. Pastor Caver and Mr. Henry talked forever. I assumed that parent/teacher conferences were unique for my inner-city school, so I think this was a pleasant experience for him. Whenever Pastor Caver did something in the community that was newsworthy, Mr. Henry acknowledged it and cut the articles out of the newspaper. At the end of that year, it was clear to me that I should become an English teacher. I made straight A's in English, and my teacher was a graduate of Yale.

I was impressed with myself. I thought maybe I was gifted in English. I knew I wanted to be a teacher; and my experience with Mr. Henry was the catalyst to assist me in narrowing down the subject. The next year when I was no longer in his class, I asked Mr. Henry for a recommendation for a scholarship. He was delighted that I asked him, so not only did he complete the letter, he went the extra mile by hand delivering it because he wanted to ensure it didn't get lost in the mail. I learned this many years later. God has always been in the details of my life, and Mr. Gordon Henry played a huge role.

CHAPTER 20

THE LITTLE GIRL ON THE COVER

I was considered the fat one because my sister and I always wore the same size except I wore the "regular" size while Denise wore the "slim" fit. Also, I hit puberty at a very early age. By the time I was in the third grade, I looked like a curvy little lady. My breasts were developing, and I was extremely self-conscience of them, especially when Hazel Womack said to me, "The reason your titties are so big is because you let men play with them." I was mortified. I had a hard time accepting my body. I thought people hated me because of my shape. However, my mom made me feel better about my appearance because she thought it was pretty. My figure looked like an hourglass. She talked about how beautiful my legs were; she thought I was shaped like her. Other little girls weren't growing at the same rate as I was. My older sister wasn't developing as quickly as I was, either. My mom had "the talk" with my sister, but I started at nine while she started at sixteen. I thought there was something wrong with me.

I didn't believe I was ready to deal with these issues just yet. This caused me to become shy. I was okay with being hidden. My birth was a secret, and this affected my personality. I allowed my big sister to speak for me instead of speaking out loud for myself. I was quiet, but I was strong-willed. I didn't verbalize a lot. However, I learned to speak through my facial expressions.

I was always thinking. I continually wondered, *God, why did you put me in this family?* I didn't believe anyone had an alcoholic mom, a grandmother who didn't like him or her, and a father who didn't even care if he or she existed. Well, maybe the father thing was more common, but that didn't change the fact that I wanted a father. I didn't open up to many because I didn't want anyone to know about my embarrassing secret, my family. If no one knew I existed, they wouldn't ask any questions. I tried to do everything perfectly, so that I would remain under the radar.

However, I worked hard in school daily in order to attract positive attention. I waited anxiously until the end of the school year in hopes of being rewarded for my efforts. To my dismay, I never won anything other than the perfect attendance award. I wasn't the smartest, but I continued to work hard to get recognized. I had a B average, and I was ranked 55 out of about 500 students in high school. I strived to be in the top 10 percent, but I was in the top 20 percent. I ran track hoping to receive a track scholarship to pay for college. Yet, I wasn't the fastest, so I chose to focus on academics since that was my way out. I was always trying to be the best, but I fell short frequently. Frustrated, I was desperate to be noticed for something good. I even sang in the church. I wanted to be a prolific singer like Rolissa Roger or Shanette Washington; they were prodigies, but I was average.

One day my hard work paid off. I never knew that filling out paperwork for college would be so rewarding. When I received my acceptance letter from the University of North Texas and a scholarship from a local church, I was overjoyed. I would get to walk across the stage at my graduation as they announced how much scholarship money I acquired. I was also excited about wearing my yellow rope that signified that I was "smart." Enthusiasm filled my room as I thought about finally being recognized for my hard work. I put on my graduation dress and my fancy heels, all inspired by this occasion.

That year I started experimenting with dating a church boy who later become my boyfriend. I was impressed by his ability to quote scriptures; I thought this was attractive. He was going to attend the graduation along with the Cavers and my sister. I also invited my mom, who I hadn't seen in a few years now. I knew she would be so proud, but she showed up filthy drunk on my big day. I just wanted to hide under a rock because my family managed to embarrass me again. I introduced my boyfriend to my staggering, slurred-speaking mom who smelled of cheap beer. This disgusting smell made me want to vomit. I was ready to go before the night got worse, but I had to graduate. I couldn't believe that she didn't stay sober for my important day. When the graduation was over, I wanted to go home to escape this nightmare, so that's what I did. After the event, I sat in my room puzzled by the questions that filled my head. *Why did she have to ruin my day? Why couldn't she stay sober for once? What did my "ex-boyfriend" think?* I couldn't face him after that night. I thought, *She can't come to another event of mine if she isn't sober.*

CHAPTER 21

MY COLLEGE DREAM
COMES TRUE

AFTER a few months passed, it was time for me to attend college, so we packed the van with my newly bought bedding and clothes. I rode in the back seat of the church van. Pastor Caver drove down Highway I-35 at snail-like speed, but it seemed like lightning speed in my mind. All of my belongings filled that space, and I was afraid and excited at the same time. The forty-five-minute drive was nerve wracking, but we had finally made it to my all girls' dorm, Maple Hall.

I wondered, *Will my roommate and suitemates like me?* I was extremely shy and believed most people didn't like me because my personality was too strong, so I braced myself for rejection. We parked in the front parking lot. Then, Pastor Caver, Sister Caver, and I headed to the crosswalk facing the entrance then stood in line to obtain my key and room number. The lady at the desk said, "You'll be in room 113." I got my key along with a welcome packet and strolled outside to gather my items.

I don't really remember what order we got the things

out of the van because fear set in. I thought, *I'm going to be here all alone. Do I have what it takes to make it in college? I've never gone to school with white people before. Am I really smart or just smart among black kids? I hope my roommate likes black people.* As we walked through the hallway, my mind was having a field day.

Finally, we arrived at room 113, and I opened the door. Suddenly, I noticed that my roommate had already set up her side of the room. I laid my baggage down and began looking at her pictures, trying to get a glimpse of her. While admiring her comforter, I noticed that she had a stuffed animal that read: I Love Jesus. That was comforting. With a smile, I resumed transporting boxes into my room. It seemed like it only took about an hour. Then, they hugged me and left me all by myself. I couldn't believe they didn't stay around to help me get my room together. Immediately, I was depressed; I had to face the college world alone.

I stayed in the room for days only leaving to eat. Eventually, one day I met two sisters who were from my hometown. While I sat there eating, one of the friendly sisters came over to me and said, "Come and join us. Don't sit over here by yourself." I agreed, so I took my tray to the next table. I learned that Petrice was a sophomore, and Wendy was a freshman like me. The oldest sister was a member of the North Texas Voices of Praise. I knew I was going to join the gospel choir when

I was in high school. I attended numerous Texas A&M's Gospel Fests while Michelle and Dimitri participated, so there was no question in my mind about joining the gospel choir. I highly anticipated the first meeting. We discussed attending choir rehearsal. We were extremely excited.

As we continued to talk, Petrice and I discovered that we had even more in common. We had been dating the same guy this spring. This was the boyfriend who attended my graduation. He took her to a family event while I was sitting at home waiting for him to arrive, but he was a no-show. This was the first indication that he was not a quality individual. He used to quote scriptures out of context to promote his wrongdoing. In the back of my mind, I thought, *The next guy I dated would be in for a treat because he would have to deal with me and all of my insecurities, family problems, and now the memories of my ex-boyfriend's misdeed.* The conversation was enlightening, as well as it gave me a glimpse of how close I would become to the two sisters. Meeting new people felt great!

CHAPTER 22

NORTH TEXAS VOICES OF PRAISE (V.O.P)

I T is amazing to think about the first meeting of Voices of Praise. I had been anticipating this day since I set foot on campus. I couldn't wait to join the choir; besides, I had seen Voices of Praise at Texas A&M's Gospel Fests. It was about 6:50 p.m., and I left my dorm with a little pep in my step. I walked on the sidewalk from Maple Hall a little before dusk until I made it to the Methodist Student Center. I reached the stairs, and I went upward to the flat surface where the center sat on an incline.

When I opened the door, I saw red carpet that reminded me of the first time I attended World Missionary Baptist Church. The place was exceptionally quiet and peaceful. However, I heard some talking, so I opened the door on the left. Someone was standing on what looked like a small stage making announcements. Later, I determined she must have been the president. The room was half full with about thirty people. I found an empty seat. I thought, *There are cute guys everywhere. You know that's important. Wow . . . and they were Christians!!! What a nice selection. Yay . . . I like college already. Ooooh . . . look at him. Focus, Shannon! You're here to sing and get closer to God. Well, I need to get my Mrs. degree too. Where are Wendy and Petrice?* I scanned the room, and I saw Wendy in the soprano section, and Petrice was on the other side with the altos. After the president finished the announcements, the pianist began to play a warm-up song. Next, he started playing songs I had heard on KHVN, the local gospel radio station in the Dallas-Fort Worth area. He was amazing, and they had a drummer too! Way cool. The choir began to sing, and it was simply angelic. I was blown away by the talent in the room. This huge football player guy named Rondy started singing a solo, and he sounded like a recording artist. This place was musical heaven. At the end of rehearsal, I looked behind me and about thirty more people had come in late. It seemed like rehearsal ended in a flash, and I was already anticipating the next rehearsal. V.O.P. became a sorority to me. I attended every rehearsal and traveled all over singing gospel tunes.

After two years, I became vice president. Not because I wanted to. There were only a few members left. People graduated and stopped participating. They became involved in other things. We were down to about twenty members when the president said, "Shannon, I need to meet with you." I was a bit skeptical. I walked upstairs to her dorm room, and she said it again, "I need to talk to you about something." I thought, *Okay, that's why I'm here.* She said, "I'm leaving school, so I need you to become the president." I thought, *I don't put myself into vulnerable situations. I'll pass.* "You're vice president," she reminded me. I was so scared. I had done a great job of staying hidden. I replied, "Okay," knowing that I would have to depend on God a lot. I finished her term and was voted in the next year. The choir grew, and our bond was amazing. V.O.P. was like family. We were a radical group for God; we weren't ashamed of our beliefs. Being in the North Texas Voices of Praise pushed me to the next level in leadership and spiritually.

CHAPTER 23

COLLEGE CLASSES

IT'S hard to believe, but I had a difficult time passing the TASP Test, which was the college entrance exam. Some people struggle with standardized tests, and I was one of those people. I remember taking a special English class that didn't count toward graduation. The purpose was simply to prepare me for this standardized test. Daily the teacher gave the class practice tests. I failed the tasks miserably. I didn't understand because I had always done well in English. That was my strength. In frustration, I called Pastor Caver and shared my problem with him. He replied, "I can help you. I'll pick you up this weekend."

He and Sister Caver came to rescue me that Friday evening. I missed them so much, and I recall that ride vividly. I guess I was talking too much, so it was obvious I had changed. I sounded like my new friends. My suitemates and roommate had been correcting my spoken grammar. I could write correctly, but I didn't use proper grammar when speaking. I'm glad they helped me because I was planning to be an English teacher;

therefore, I welcomed the educational critiques of my oral language. Pastor Caver asked me to be quiet because I was talking nonstop from the point I got into the car. I was definitely much different than before. When I left, I was almost mute, and my dialect had changed. We made it home, and I went to bed immediately. I was exhausted.

The next morning while I sat at the kitchen table Pastor Caver showed me an easy method of writing a paper. He created an outline and discussed the details that should be included. I was amazed at the simple process, but I was a bit irritated with my teacher. I passed the TASP Test during the next administration with flying colors.

The following semester, I enrolled in regular classes. The first week was unforgettable. I remember eating breakfast in Kerr's cafeteria. Then, I put on my cute black coat with the plaid lining and journeyed to my inaugural English college class. As I walked uneasily down the pavement, I thought, *Can I do this?* Finally, I went into the Lyceum, and that's when I realized it was an auditorium. There were about 500 students in this class. I found my seat in the crowd. Overwhelmed, I wondered, *How will I be able to ask a question? How will my teacher know I exist?* The lights were turned off, and the professor walked to the stage. My immediate thought was, *This is going to be boring.* The teacher began to ramble from the start, and I took a mental excursion. He said read chapters one through three before the next class, and I almost passed out. This book was huge, and I felt doomed because I hated reading. A little discouraged, I left class hoping for a more uplifting sociology class.

There were about sixty people in that session. This class was smaller, but the professor told us to read four chapters and prepare for a quiz on Wednesday, which was the next class. I was in big trouble because it appeared college was simply a bunch of reading classes. I began to wonder, *How am I going to graduate?* Also, I got angry with my previous educational institution because the curriculum didn't prepare me for the rigor of college academics. I wished someone had forced me to read more.

As I struggled that semester, it seemed that most students had already read the assigned stories in their high school English classes, and I hadn't read a novel in its entirety. I was concerned. I began to watch the girl who sat in front of me who always received A's on every assignment. I noticed that she was writing notes on the side of each paragraph. This is when I had an epiphany. She was writing down the main idea. I thought, *That's what they meant by that all of these years. I get it; she's writing down the main ideas. That's how she's passing and ensuring she is comprehending what she's reading.* I wished someone had shown me this strategy before now. My reading skills interfered with my success, but eventually I adapted to my educational environment. I maintained a GPA good enough to keep my scholarship and financial aid. I was grateful to have this opportunity to make my dreams come true. God never left me. Things may have gotten rough, but he always saw me through.

CHAPTER 24

I FINALLY MEET MY FATHER

WHEN I was twenty-two, I desired to meet my dad. Watching Oprah find people's missing relatives on her talk show inspired me to locate my father. I lived with many questions for years. I knew that my pastor would help me, so I solicited him to assist me. I was extremely afraid because I didn't know how my father was going to respond. Pastor Caver asked me various questions. The two most important questions were "What is his name?" and "Where did he live last?"

I didn't know, so I called my mom and asked her the questions. She responded, "Fat Daddy is his nickname. He lived in Royce, Texas years ago." Then, she pleaded with me not to call him. I replied, "Thank you" and relayed the information to my pastor. She had hidden this information from me long enough. As Pastor Caver picked up the phone and started calling people in Royce, Texas, I reflected on the many times my grandmother talked about how worthless he was, but I wanted to find out for myself.

Eventually, Pastor Caver reached one of father's

aunts, and she told him where he lived. She also gave him his full name and said he lived in Terrell, Texas. My stomach began to hurt because I knew the next call would be to Frank Johnson. As he dialed the number, I felt like I was going to lose my breakfast. I listened as Pastor Caver asked him questions like "Do you know a woman by the name of Caroline Baker? Did you have a relationship with her? Well, I know a young lady who believes you are her father, and she would like to meet you."

Frank said he knew my mother, and he did believe that I was his daughter. He also said he would love to meet me, but his family was concerned that I might be violent. Therefore, they wanted me to meet them in Terrell, Texas at their home.

That day is cemented in my memory. It was a sunny spring break day when we piled into the car. Pastor and Sister Caver took me to meet the mysterious man and his family. His family said, "They were afraid that I would be violent." No, I should be afraid. I was possibly breaking up a happy home. I would be meeting his children, who were devastated by their father's infidelity. How would they receive me? I wasn't the one who caused this problem. I simply represented the act. As we passed the barren land and dusty roads, I felt a huge knot in my stomach, and I began to sweat and feel queasy. We had to pull over while I released my nervousness in chunks of liquid on the side of the road. I cleaned myself up and felt a lot better. I was preparing to meet my father after all of these years.

We drove up to the light blue wooden house with a couple of cars outside. The Cavers and I got out of the car and walked to the porch of the house. While I was almost fully paralyzed by fear, I kept moving. Pastor Caver knocked on the door, and we walked into the living room. To my surprise, everyone said hello and hugged me. His wife was first, and then I met my three beautiful sisters. I discussed my birthday with my new sisters, and we realized our mothers were pregnant at the same time. The girls seemed somewhat shattered by the news, but they were welcoming and kind. I could see the disappointment on their faces as they glared at their dad.

Mrs. Johnson was extremely gracious. She said she had known about us for years. One of my father's friends told her about my sister and me once when he was drunk. I thought, *What, my sister and me? You must be mistaken my sister's father is someone else.* She looked at me with great conviction and continued to say, "Your sister is Fat Daddy's child too." I didn't want to believe it, but my sister was his child as well. I discovered another secret.

That's why my mother adamantly told me not to find him. I was disappointed because she had a "father" all of this time, and now that I found mine, I have to share him. My mom lied to that poor guy and my sister. She thought that was her dad, but as I think about it I never thought she looked anything like him. However, Denise resembled "my" daddy. This was all extremely overwhelming.

While being in Terrell, Texas, I noticed something else. They had a lot more than we did. My father owned an auto mechanic shop. He also collected old vehicles and made $100,000 once he gathered 100 cars. He had a small farm with cows and pigs. He had been working at his job for years, and he seemed to have money saved because he was frugal. This made me fume because we struggled, and my mom didn't ask for one dime since she promised to keep us a secret. He seemed to be grateful to my mother for keeping her word. After that day, I felt like I uncovered what I needed to know, but I didn't need a father anymore. I would never be daddy's little girl because my parents deprived me of that. However, I was thankful for the scripture that states in Psalms 27:10, "Though my father and mother forsake me, the Lord will receive me." Mr. J and Pastor Caver filled that father role for me, and my real father could never measure up to my God-given fathers. Mr. J was there until he died, and after his death, Pastor Howard Caver finished the job. Because of how God used them,

I never felt like a fatherless child. Thank you Father God for always looking out for me.

CHAPTER 25

V.O.P.'s Vice-President

I worked with a small group of officers while being the president of North Texas Voices of Praise. The organization struggled to raise money, but when Daren Wilson became vice president, the money problems dissipated. He knew how to fund raise. Once we did a concession stand fund-raiser and made about $10,000. That was a record-breaking amount for our small organization. I was impressed with his ability to obtain money.

He and I became good friends. When we didn't have dates, we hung out with each other. We frequently went to the movies and fast food restaurants. I was just having fun with my "little brother". He was younger than me. We even went on a double date. He brought his girlfriend, and I went with another male friend. We worked out together too. We harmonized in the car. I remember singing "Silver and Gold" by Kirk Franklin in my red Chevy Spectrum. I talked to him about the guy or guys I liked. He drove my car occasionally, but I didn't like him romantically.

Everyone used to say, "Y'all are going to get married."

I didn't understand why they would say that. Besides, I had a warped idea about marriage because of my experiences. Remember, my biological father was a married man and so was Mr. J. If that's what marriage consisted of, I didn't want any part of it. I would only get married if the guy wouldn't cheat on me, so I asked God to send me someone who loved him more than he loved me. Then, I knew I could trust him.

Also, I was afraid that I would hurt him since I had all of those hidden issues, but were they hidden from him? We talked about everything. He became my best friend. Since Daren and I were such good friends, I asked him to escort me to the Baptist Student Union Pageant. I planned on singing and sharing my story in that arena. I felt like God wanted me to do that. I thought, *Really, you want me to share something so personal in front of all of these people?* However, I was prepared to be obedient while being terrified. I waited backstage with him before they presented us. Incapacitated by fear, I stood next to Daren trembling as I thought about uncovering my secrets. I tried to block everything out, not realizing that they were ruling my life. While standing there, I found it pretty amazing how God took me from hiding in a closet as my mom tried to kill me to a pageant on stage in Tennessee. Next, Daren took my hands and said, "Let me pray for you." I almost melted; the fear disappeared. The prayer was beautiful. That was the day I thought

I knew who he was. God had revealed my Knight in Shining Armor. He knew my flaws because I had shared them with him as a friend. After that, I thought he would have been the perfect boyfriend, but it simply didn't happen.

CHAPTER 26

GRADUATION

I struggled with leaving college since it was such a pleasant experience for me. Life became what I thought normal should be. I was a campus leader as a resident assistant at Kerr Hall and president of North Texas Voices of Praise. I hid behind the Caver family as my own. My "father" was a pastor and my siblings graduated from Texas A&M. I was "somebody". However as graduation grew closer, I wondered if my mom was going to show up and embarrass me again, so in order to guard myself, I called my sister and asked her to tell Mama not to come to my ceremony if she wasn't sober that day. I speculated whether she would be able to honor my request or if that precious liquid was more important than me. It seemed that I had lost out for years to this magic potion. I began to think about the horror that took place years ago. Nervously, I contemplated my accomplishment; I had defied a lot of odds. I was going to be the first person to complete college in my family. I was getting a degree in Interdisciplinary Studies with a minor in English. I was confident that the Cavers and my sister would be there, but I wasn't sure about my mom. *I thought,* Was she going to appear and reveal all of the shame I'd tried to erase and block out of my mind? I had done an excellent job of hiding my secrets in college. What was going to happen on my special day? Would I be embarrassed one more time?

I recall getting ready around noon because I was graduating at two. I put on my professional-looking black dress with five white circular-ring patterns sewn around the neck area. My outfit was completed with some elegant black sling-back heels. I enjoyed dressing up. It made me feel like I could take on the world. I needed an extra dose of assurance that day. With my cap and gown in my hand, I left my dorm room and jumped in my car. I talked to God the whole way. My nerves tried to take over; however, I had to be strong. I hadn't seen my mom in about four years. I really didn't want to see her. Or did I? She frustrated me so much; therefore, I braced myself to be disappointed or uncomfortable. I knew she had failed numerous times before, but I wanted her to finally support me and make me proud.

I arrived at the coliseum to line up on the sidewalk and enter the tunnel wearing my black cap and gown. The graduates had to line up in accordance to our previous practice. While I waited and chatted, I heard, "Shannon! Shannon! Shannon!" I turned around, and it was my big sister, Denise, screaming my name. I could tell she was so proud of me as she beamed. I didn't see anyone else. I waved at her and began to walk into the tunnel. I entered the coliseum with what seemed to be thousands of other people all dressed like me. That day I felt special. I had achieved my goal of attending college, and I was on my way to fulfilling my aspiration of becoming a teacher. I had a flashback to second grade where the dream started. I didn't know how I was going to get here, but here I was with my cap and gown flowing as I strolled to my seat. I was tremendously proud of myself. I had proven that through adversity I could still be successful. Only God could make a Baker successful. I hadn't seen anyone else reach this level in my family. At that moment, I realized how many people God had assigned to me to ensure that I achieved my dream. I sat down envisioning all of the people who encouraged me, but I'm not sure what the speakers spoke about. I do remember my name being called and walking across the stage to receive just a few seconds of fame. It was all worth it. That piece of paper made my chest stick out. I was a college graduate! When I exited the coliseum, I looked for my family. I located Pastor Caver, Sister Caver, Denise, Marcus, Shomie, Sister Sharon, and Brother Westbrook. My mother wasn't there. She couldn't put the bottle down that day. My sister told me that she was intoxicated, so she couldn't make it.

I was relieved, but disappointed at the same time.

My mom managed to take my special day and make it a sad moment. However, I was glad God never left me because I knew that this little girl wouldn't have graduated without him watching over her. I learned to call on him in difficult times, so my relationship had gotten stronger year after year. Still, there was a lot I didn't understand. *Who misses their child's major life event like that? God, why was I born in this family?*

CHAPTER 27

LIFE AFTER GRADUATION

I was a little disappointed that I didn't have any prospects for marriage. I figured I would just date and have a great time. Besides, I was an attractive single college graduate with no kids. I had a nice apartment. Who wouldn't find me amazing? I began dating a few guys, and it was truly a waste of time. But, I was having fun, or so I thought.

One Saturday everything changed. I had to travel to Denton, Texas in order to pick up some furniture my friend was giving me. She was practically providing me with a whole new living room of furniture. I was excited because it was such a blessing. I had made arrangements with CT, Daren's roommate, to help move the items. I rented a truck, and my friend and I were headed to CT's apartment so that he could help us gather the items.

When we arrived at his apartment, I knocked on the door. Surprisingly, CT wasn't there. He went to play basketball with some friends. I couldn't believe that he would forget that he had agreed to help me. While I found out CT wasn't available, his roommate volunteered by saying, "I'll help you!" I was in shock because I didn't see Daren as the handy type. He was more of a "pretty boy". He made sure that everything was in place. He was always well put together. I'm sure he cleaned or polished his shoes each night. The idea of him getting a little dirty didn't correlate with Daren's persona. However, he jumped into the U-Haul with Miko and me as we headed to the storage unit to collect the furniture. After about thirty minutes of loading the things in the truck, we went to Fort Worth. It took us about forty-five minutes to get there.

We reached the Carol Oaks Apartment complex and entered the security gate that didn't always work, and we drove to the back of the complex. I jumped out of the truck to unlock my upstairs apartment door. Next, Daren, Miko, and I picked up the sofa and began to take the journey upstairs. Placing the sofa at an angle to get inside the door was sort of tricky, but we ultimately figured it out. Getting the love seat upstairs was easier. After delivering the furniture, we sweated profusely as we discussed what we were going to eat in that cozy apartment. My small abode looked terrific with the new furnishings.

Eventually, we decided that we wanted hamburgers, so Daren and I sluggishly strolled to the U-Haul to return it and get dinner. Miko followed us in her car. We parked and walked inside the establishment to fill out the final paper work in order to return the truck. Next, Miko drove us to Wendy's. We went inside to order our meals and sat down to eat. While we ate, we talked about school and church. Then, Miko and I took Daren back to Denton. When we reached Daren's apartment, CT was there. I was a little upset that he didn't help, so I gave him one of my disappointed faces and some uncomfortable vibes. I was extremely appreciative of Daren; therefore, it really didn't matter. I soon learned that Daren's help was a divine appointment.

CHAPTER 28

ALL MOVED IN

WOULD you believe that after Daren helped me move into my apartment he began coming to hang out with me each weekend? I cancelled several dates because Daren would spontaneously announce that he was coming to visit me. I knew I would have more fun with him, so I didn't hesitate to cancel the dates. I felt comfortable with him; he was like family. However, I started to get suspicious after a while because I was spending a great deal of time with him. When I talked to other guys about our friendship, they didn't believe that we could just be friends, but we were. I began comparing the guys I was dating with Daren, and they didn't meet my standards. His relationship with God was stronger than any guy I had ever dated. I told Miko about my suspicions, and we agreed I should ask him if he liked me romantically. I planned on escorting him to a wedding that upcoming Saturday, so I intended to ask him to reveal his heart at that time.

When Saturday arrived, I started getting ready around five. I put on my navy green-colored dress with gold heels. I wore my hair in a roller set and finalized my attire with a gold necklace. I knew I looked great, as usual. I was anxious and excited. I heard Daren knocking at the door. I opened the door, and he was wearing a black suit with a gold-patterned tie. He always dressed exquisitely, so he looked absolutely stunning.

We traveled to a nearby Catholic church in Arlington, Texas. I think the wedding was beautiful, but I was too focused on the question I had to ask that night. After the wedding, we went to the reception at a quaint upscale restaurant in a skyscraper on the top floor. We engaged in small talk with others attending the event. Typically, I was serious, but Daren always made me laugh. His sense of humor was comforting. After being seated, we began consuming the meal. I thought about how I was going to confront him at the end of the night. Following the reception, we traveled to Daren's car in order to return to my apartment. When we were getting close to my apartment, I asked, "Are you trying to like me or something? I've been spending a lot of time with you. I've postponed and cancelled dates because I've been hanging out with you."

I could see the awkwardness in his eyes as he said, "What do you think?" in a nervous sort of way. Daren possessed an innocence that I found refreshing. He wasn't all used up and experienced, unlike the other young men I had dated. I was relieved because I thought this might actually work. He was perfect as a best friend; however, I wasn't sure about as a boyfriend. I didn't want to destroy our relationship, but what if it worked? Besides, he knew all of my secrets anyway. I believe he was the only person who knew everything, and he didn't think I was a freak. He actually thought I was pretty incredible.

Well, I guess we were officially dating, but we didn't want everybody involved in our business; therefore, we kept it a secret. I reflected back to a conversation I had with Cynthia, a friend from church. Oh no . . . she was right. She said that we were going to get married, and I said, "No, Daren is just my friend." Also, Daren's ex-girlfriend is going to think that I told her not to pursue him because I wanted him for myself, which wasn't the case. I believe everyone else could see that we were meant to be together way before we did.

From that point on, Daren traveled to Fort Worth each weekend to see me. I was delighted that God had rescued me from the frustrating dating world because no one could match Daren in character, appearance, personality, style, drive, and intelligence. I realized later that I had been using him as a measuring stick, and no one was measuring up because there was only one, Daren Alex Wilson.

CHAPTER 29

FIRST OFFICIAL DATE

H E came to Fort Worth as usual. I heard the knock at my apartment door, but this time it was different. This situation was serious; Daren and I were dating. I had to dress properly and carry myself like a lady. Or did I? Well, it was just Daren, and I didn't have to be fake. He knew me already. This sure did complicate things, but I was willing to take the risk.

We had planned to go shopping, so we drove to Hulen Mall. I recall walking on the second floor, and we passed a jewelry store. Daren said, "Let's look." I agreed to enter, so he asked me to pick out the rings I liked. Wow! That sure was interesting, but I didn't take this seriously because it was our first date. *"A little unique and amusing,"* I thought.

Daren and I continued to date for weeks. Those weeks turned into about three months when Daren asked me what was my favorite restaurant, and I replied, "The Magic Time Machine."

He responded, "Let's go this weekend!"

I answered, "Okay." I was overly excited. I hoped I

still enjoyed the restaurant because it was my favorite when I was fourteen, but now I was twenty-three. All week, I anticipated the date to my favorite restaurant. Daren traveled from Denton as usual. I heard the knock at my door that I had become accustomed to for the last three months. I opened the door, and there he was looking as handsome as ever. His caramel brown skin seemed to sparkle when he smiled. He always made me light up. He caused me to laugh until it hurt, my personal comedian. I grabbed my things and headed to his white Ford Taurus. He wasn't as playful and silly tonight. I asked him if he was okay because he didn't seem like himself. He said he was fine. We finally arrived at the Magic Time Machine, and my heart fluttered with excitement.

When we walked in, I realized I had outgrown the restaurant, but we had come all of this way. I would simply enjoy it. The hostess seated us, and our character, Captain Ahab from Moby Dick, said he was going to be our waiter. He took the drink order while we looked over the menu. When the waiter returned, we ordered our food. We talked about our week for a while, and then our food arrived.

Daren became quiet again and just wasn't himself. I wondered if Daren was going to break up with me. While his odd behavior continued to concern me, the waiter appeared and announced to the restaurant that

Daren wanted to ask me something. I was in total shock. He pulled out this beautiful ring that he designed for me. The ring had a huge marquis diamond in the middle with red rubies. He described how the rubies represented our relationship being covered by the blood of Jesus. Daren put a great deal of thought into creating my ring. The jeweler created it from a drawing he made. I guess he had been paying on it since our first date. He said, "Shannon, will you marry me?"

I didn't say anything because I was paralyzed with joy. I put the ring on, and the lady at another table asked, "Did she say yes?"

I replied, "Yes." I was astonished at how fast God moved.

When I got home, I immediately called my family. First, I reached out to my God-given father, Pastor Caver, who said that Daren had come to the church office earlier in the week and asked him if he could marry me, so he gave him his blessing. I thought, *Wow, how could he do all of that without me knowing?* Next, I contacted my sister, and she couldn't believe I was getting married. She thought I would remain single forever. I thought she believed I was too mean to get married and that no one would be attracted to my unique personality. Even I knew it would definitely take a special man because I wasn't going to settle for anything less than God's best, and Daren was that. Finally, I called my friends, and they were excited.

Daren and I were engaged for a year. I believe God can do exceedingly above what you can ask or think, and that's what he did when he selected Daren for me. (Ephesians 3:20)

CHAPTER 30

DAY OF ANSWERED PRAYER

IT'S amazing to think about my important day, and nothing was going to go wrong because I had been planning perfection for a year. Also, my friend, Natalie Dyer, volunteered to coordinate the ceremony. I didn't care whether my mom showed up or not. This was my Cinderella moment, and I had been praying for my happily ever after for years.

Without a doubt Daren Alex Wilson was perfectly crafted for me; he had proven himself as a friend. I watched him date others, and I knew he would be faithful. I needed someone I could honor and respect. He came from an excellent family. His father was an NFL coach, and Mrs. Wilson worked in the Social Work Department at the University of Minnesota. Veronica graduated from Vanderbilt University with a degree in engineering, and she was about to attend medical school. His little brother Trey was an outstanding athlete at Stanford University. Our families were complete opposites.

As I thought about the family dynamics, I reflected back to the rehearsal dinner. I remember my mom meeting Mrs. Wilson for the first time. While they said hello, Mrs. Wilson asked my mom if my dad would be attending. Daren's mom didn't realize she was pulling off a scab. I believe my mom paused and said, "I'm not sure," with a little irritation on her face. I'm certain she wished she were drunk at that moment. Later, she told me his mom asked too many questions. The real problem was she was uncovering a secret, one that she hadn't dealt with in twenty-five years until now.

My mind returned to the special day. I began to gather my wedding dress, shoes, and undergarments while preparing to head to the Lena Pope Chapel. I walked out of the door and placed my things in my black Acura Integra. I knew my wedding was going to be a dream come true.

When I arrived at the chapel, the makeup artist was there. We walked down the path while admiring the greenery that surrounded the area. The place was absolutely exquisite. I opened the doors of the venue, and I envisioned my big day as we approached the basement area. I placed my dress bag on the hook and set my container of accessories in the bridal room. The make-up artist/hair stylist settled into her space. Then, I joined her eagerly to get started. She used these fancy electric curlers to style my hair. Next, she created a beautiful, natural look on my face. She simply enhanced my everyday appearance with make-up. Typically, I didn't wear cosmetics. Now, I was ready to transform into my version of Cinderella.

I pranced over to my bridal gown, excited about the day. I unzipped the dress bag and removed the garment. When I first laid eyes on this form-fitting, beaded gown in *Bride* magazine, I knew it would fit me perfectly, and I was right. I only tried on one dress during my search. There it was on the hanger, waiting on me. I stepped into my girdle and put on my special bra. I pulled the dress over my legs and up toward the upper part of my body. I looked like a modern day African-American Cinderella as elegant and gorgeous as I had dreamed. I thought, *Thank you God for hearing my prayers all of these years.* I was elated. This day was going to be magical in my eyes. I put my earrings on while Sister Caver came to my room to check on me and tell me how beautiful I looked. She also stated that the photographer wanted to take pictures of me with the flower girl and junior bridesmaid. Charity and LaShominique walked into the room looking adorable. Charity wore a miniature wedding dress, and Shomie wore a toddler's version of the bridesmaids dress. The photographer positioned us for the brief photo shoot.

After that, I remained downstairs while everyone was transitioning upstairs to begin. While waiting in the dressing room, I thanked God for everything. I tried not to cry because I didn't want to mess up my makeup, but

God had done so much. I was pretty choked up when Natalie announced, "It's time!"

I walked upstairs with a smile on my face and a song in my heart, although a little nervous. When I got there, the flower girl and ring bearer were gently dropping flower petals on the white runway. Next, little Shomie began ringing a bell and saying loudly, "The bride is coming! The bride is coming!" and running to her place next to the bridesmaids.

Finally, Mr. Villareal, a colleague from Stripling Middle School, began playing "Here Comes the Bride" on his trumpet along with Dimitri, who played the piano. God's presence could be felt strongly as the sunlight glistened through the skylights while Pastor Caver walked me down the aisle. I gracefully sobbed as I strolled. When we reached the altar, Pastor Davis, our college pastor, asked, "Who gives this woman to be wed?" The Cavers and my mom replied, "We do." Daren then took my arm, and Pastor Caver joined Pastor Davis on the stage. There was no way that anyone else was going to perform my ceremony because he had been there through my spiritual journey. Our college pastor began the ceremony, and Pastor Caver completed the ceremony with the vows.

Pastor Davis exchanged positions with Pastor Caver. After switching places, Pastor Caver said, "First they're going to sing a song to each other." We sang "Always"

by Atlantic Starr. Daren sang flawlessly, but when it was
my turn, I was so nervous I cracked a little bit. Once I
heard myself, I adjusted, and my vocals improved when
I sang the next line. Some of the guests began to tear up
because the lyrics were perfect. Next, Pastor Caver said,
"The couple has created their own vows. First, Daren
will repeat after me.

Daren's vows:
I commit myself to you this day,
To love, honor, and cherish you,
To strengthen, guide, and nurture you,
To protect, comfort, and provide for you,
In good times and in bad times,
In health and wealth,
Under all circumstances,
From now until death part us,
So now help me God.

My vows were repeated with sobs between words:
With all that I have, I do love you,
I respect you as the leader of the household,
I am blessed that God chose you for me,
I honor your relationship with Christ,
And with that I will not contend,
Through all of your endeavors, I will support you.
I will do nothing that will bring shame to you,
When there are storms in our lives,

Know that I am beside you,
And I will never leave you alone.
God has given me a priceless prince.
I prayed since I was a little girl for Mr. Right,
And here you stand.
You know that I love you,
And I will strive to be the wife God would have me
to be.

Finally, we completed our vows with traditional oaths. The preacher said, "I now pronounce you husband and wife. You may now kiss your bride." Daren lifted up my veil and planted his lips on mine. Pastor Caver said, "May I be the first to present to you, Mr. and Mrs. Daren Alex Wilson." With huge smiles, we exited and the guests were told to go to the Botanical Gardens for the reception. We remained there and had pictures taken. Everything else we did was a blur because we had to leave immediately after the reception and head to the airport. I recall walking through the bubbles as the guests blew them while we exited the venue. Now, my fairy tale was about to begin in the Bahamas.

CHAPTER 31

MY HAPPILY EVER AFTER

EVERYTHING seemed perfect, my husband woke up at five o'clock each morning to worship God and read his Bible before leaving for work. He was who I thought he was, a devout man of God, and he was in love with me. God had exceeded my expectations for a mate. We lived in our new apartment in the Arlington area of Texas. I worked at Stripling Middle School in Fort Worth as a language arts teacher, and he was an account executive at a prominent advertising agency in Dallas. I was living my dream, until . . .

I had to face an episode that arose shortly before our wedding. The left side of my body became numb. I experienced very little feeling in the left side of my mouth and dragged my left leg because I didn't possess the full range of motion. This occurred for approximately three weeks. I was very concerned, so I scheduled a doctor's appointment. I went to a neurologist, and the medical staff administered an EKG and CAT scan to determine my fate. The doctor told me what he suspected, so he gave me some videos to watch in preparation for the disability. He stated that he would call me at work in a few days with the results. I recall it was a standard-ized testing day when the doctor called. I remember the school secretary contacting my room over the intercom, "Mrs. Wilson! Mrs. Wilson, you have a phone call in the office." This happened as I was about to pass out the tests. As fear came over my body, someone came to my room to watch my students while I walked to the office and the secretary said, "Pick up line 1," as I entered the front door. The doctor was on the phone. He said without care, "Hello, Mrs. Wilson. I have the results from your tests. It was as I suspected. You have Multiple Sclerosis. Set up an appointment, so that we can treat this illness."

Traumatized, I began to cry, and I asked the secretary could I speak to the principal. I shared the information with the principal in between sniffles and told her that I had to go home. I wouldn't be able to administer the test this way. I called my husband, hysterical. I wished that I hadn't gotten married if he had to deal with this diag-nosis and me. We prayed and decided not to receive the doctor's diagnosis because God's word said that I was healed by his stripes, so I meditated on this and decided not to return to the doctor. Many people told me that I wouldn't be able to have children, and I didn't want to start taking medicine, which could put my children in harm's way.

Within seven months I was expecting a child, and I was afraid. I wasn't sure that I could be a good mother because I didn't have a good role model. I planned on having children after five years, but obviously God's plan was different. I remember being extremely angry with my husband, but I don't believe he knew because he was overjoyed. He absolutely loved kids, and he thought he would be a great father. Eventually, I got over it. Pregnancy was challenging. I felt like a Michelin man. My stomach seemed to take over my petite frame. I was cute at first, but the cuteness wore off quickly. About the sixth month, I was put on bed rest. All the while, I was afraid of how well I would perform as a mom. When we found out we were going to have a healthy little boy, I wanted to name him after Daren, but Daren didn't want him to be a junior. Therefore, his middle name would be Daren. We put a lot of thought into his first name. He purchased various baby books to select the proper name for our child who was conceived out of love. We had many names in mind, but we liked Brendan the most because it means "beacon of light." We knew that our child would be a beacon of light in this dark world.

I learned from the Cavers that a name was important. The Bible always emphasized the importance of the meaning of a name. For instance, the Bible states, "The virgin will conceive and bear a son, and they will call him *Emmanuel*," which means "God with us." We thought about the Bible when determining our son's name.

After nine uncomfortable months, it was time to deliver Brendan Daren Wilson. My C-section was scheduled for 7:30 a.m. I spent the night at the hospital in preparation for our new arrival. Unlike my pregnancy, I was excited about delivering him. Also, I was proud that we could offer him a loving home. I recall them coming into my room and saying, "Are you ready, Mrs. Wilson? It's time." I was afraid of being cut, but I was ready to meet my baby. I had been anticipating his appearance for months. The hospital staff rolled me out of the room in a bed, and my husband followed with his video camera. The anesthesiologist administered a shot into my spine, and I lost feeling in the lower parts of my body. They took me into another room where my doctor was waiting. He told me he was about to begin. Later, I heard a loud rush of liquid spilling on the floor. Next, they said, "He has a lot of hair." When they brought him close, a white substance and blood covered his pink body. My husband started filming after the doctor was finished. I was expecting the sound of his cry because I wanted to know he was okay. Finally, I heard the reassuring sound of his strong lungs. They wiped him up and wrapped him with a blanket while placing a little newborn hat on his head. He was adorable. He had thick curly hair with bronze-colored skin, and he was a little chubby. We marveled at God's creation. Daren and I felt he was a true representation of our love. I thought at that moment how could anyone abandon or mistreat his or her own creation. Immediately, I thanked God that I got the opportunity to give my son something I didn't have: parents who loved God, each other, and him. I was going to make sure that I corrected every wrong that my parents committed.

After spending two days in the hospital, we prepared to return home. I dressed Brendan in a cute little navy and sky-blue outfit. Then, we packed our bags. The nurse rolled in a wheelchair to transport me to the car. I was still in a little bit of pain after the C-section. Daren collected our things and escorted Brendan and me to the lobby. While I waited, he pulled the car close to the entrance. He returned to get us. Finally, we were on our way home.

I was a bit fearful because now I had to take care of my baby alone. Naturally, I wasn't nurturing. I assisted my sister with taking care of our cousins when we were younger, and that was a lot of work. This truly made me lose interest in babies, so I was thankful that my mother-in-law was coming to Texas to help me take care of Brendan. Besides, I was still recovering from the surgery.

After getting settled at home, Daren left and traveled

to the DFW Airport to pick up his mother. When she arrived, I was grateful because I didn't trust my mother to play this role. Daren's mom seemed to really enjoy being a grandmother. She didn't want to be Granny, Madea, or Big Mama because she was classy, so she thought "Grammy" was suitable. It fit her perfectly. She stayed in the room with Brendan and woke up with him in the middle of the night. She remained for two weeks. I will never forget the day she had to leave. I was extremely afraid. I don't believe she understood how fearful I was. I didn't think I could do it alone. I recall telling her, "I don't know what I'm going to do without you." I'm sure she thought I was just saying that like people usually do, but not me. I thought that my skills were affected by my mom's inability to parent. Now it was my turn, but I had to do it afraid.

Brendan was delightful. My husband and I poured our love into our baby, so he grew up believing he could accomplish anything. At the age of three, our amazing little toddler learned Psalm 100, and he recited it in front of an audience of five-hundred. Without any fear, this preschooler stood in front of St. Andrews Church of God in Christ with his little kid voice while a youth leader and Daren held the microphone and said, "Psalm100: 'Make a joyful noise unto the Lord . . . .'" The audience gave him a thunderous applause, and I could hear the teenagers call him a genius. I was pleased because I knew that I was raising him right.

Three years after having Brendan, I was pregnant with our daughter. Daren really wanted a little girl, but I recall being concerned about the finances. I took walks in the neighborhood to exercise, so one day while I strolled through the neighborhood, I talked to God about our situation. Then, I glanced at the ground and noticed a balled up $10 bill lying on the sidewalk. I began to cry because I knew this was my reminder that if God had to make money fall from the heavens, he was going to take care of us. That was the end of me worrying, and we welcomed a new addition to our happy family.

Daren carefully chose our daughter's name. We agreed on the name Kensley. Her name means "Queen of the Meadow". We liked this name. We knew it was our job to guide her in the path he had for her. She was absolutely gorgeous. She could have been a baby model except she wouldn't cooperate. We were once banned from the YMCA because she was a bit aggressive. She scratched another baby, and we were asked to leave. I knew she was going to be a leader, but I had to tame the queen in her. She didn't have the confidence that her brother had. This concerned me until she enrolled in gymnastics; she was a natural. Her personality and tenacity were perfect for her petite, gymnast frame.

In conclusion, God allowed me to give my children

everything I didn't have as a child. The diagnosis was a seven-year scare, but God healed me eleven years ago. My children have a supportive mother and father, stable home, consistent encouragement, and faith in God. I wasn't daddy's little girl, but my daughter is. My kids don't have a "baby daddy"; they have an amazing father. I had a rough start, but God is continuing to write the amazing end to my story. I'm extremely proud of my happy home, so I challenge those of you who come from a dysfunctional family similar to mine: Make your family the one you wanted by making decisions that will make your future child or children proud. You have the power to change everything.

CHAPTER 32

THE ANSWER TO MY QUESTION

AS a teacher, students with dysfunctional families gravitated to me. It was like they knew my history, but I hadn't told them anything. I actually thought I looked more sophisticated, using the Cavers as my family until God revealed to me that I was hiding behind them. I didn't realize I was robbing him of his glory by acting like I was a part of the Caver family. He clearly stated to me that everything that I had been able to accomplish as a Caver wasn't miraculous, but as a Baker, it was apparent that he was with me. My testimony existed in being a Baker, not in being a Caver.

So one school year, I was writing a poetry lesson plan in which the students were supposed to select poems that revealed who they were and present this information to the class. As I was writing it, God impressed upon me to tell my students my story through this assignment. I knew it had to be God because I wouldn't share this information with just anybody, but I could trust my students. I recall standing in front of my class and describing the assignment in great detail. Then, I took them to the computer lab, and they used the Internet to identify personal poetry for the next week.

As the day drew near for me to share my assignment, I became nervous. I thought, *What if they say something rude about my family? What if I can't handle it? What if I cry? I've never done this before. I don't know what will happen.* After the bell rang, I strolled to the front and said, "I'm going to demonstrate what I want you to do first. I dimmed the lights and lit some candles for our poetry slam. They snapped their fingers, and I began with "I'm sure some of you wonder why I am the way I am." They knew what that meant. Some of my students thought I would be a good prison guard. I was extremely serious about my job, but today they were going to learn about how I became this way. I started with my childhood and talked about being left alone by my mom, and the tears began to flow. My students began to cry along with me. I knew that some of my students could identify; however, others were horrified. No one laughed or said anything rude. The ones who needed to be empowered revealed their broken homes through their presentations that day. I applauded them for their bravery, and I reminded the students that they couldn't share other students' stories. I recall one young lady describing how she had been taken by Child Protective Services and that she wouldn't be able to see her parents until she was 18 per court order. I was so proud of this young lady; she shared her story at age thirteen. I told her that she was extremely courageous to do this. I shared my story, but I was in my mid-thirties. She was definitely further in the process of healing than I was. I protected her by reiterating the importance of not telling other people's stories.

From that moment, my students had a different type of respect for me. They seemed impressed that I had fought so hard to make it, and that I had become their teacher through this perseverance. I believe that they finally understood why I would respond, "Life isn't fair, so get over it!" when they complained about something not being fair or when they complained about something being too hard, I would say, "Suck it up. The world isn't going to adjust because you think something is too hard. That isn't life."

Eventually, I learned that I was born in the Baker family to inspire kids like me and let them know that they can make it. I felt tormented by my secrets and family, but God guided me through even when I thought he wasn't there. He assigned people to teach and care for me. I don't believe any of this happened by chance. It was all ordained by God. Philippians 4:13 states, "We can do all things through Christ if we rely on him for strength." Therefore, I am proud of what I've accomplished through my secret weapon, God! He gave me supernatural strength.

ROUGH AROUND THE EDGES

Imperfection is my name,
If you knew my secrets,
I'd be ashamed.

I try to hide behind,
A bowed head,
Or loud voice,
Oftentimes an awful choice,

I wish this roughness would go away,
But I can't escape them,
They haunt me from day to day.

Sometimes they reveal themselves,
When I'm not aware,
They peek their little edges out,
In places that I didn't even know they were there.

I wish the edges would go away,
They're so painful,
It hurts for them to stay.

I no longer want rough edges to reside here,
Because they complicate my life,
They create a lot of fear.

But, when I fall to my knees to pray,
God says I'll help you through the rough edges,
Your story will help someone someday!
Sandra Walters

Made in the USA
Columbia, SC
24 August 2021